Hg2 Paris

A Hedonist's guide to

Paris

Written and photographed by
Nina Vlotides

A Hedonist's guide to Rome

Managing director – Tremayne Carew Pole
Marketing director – Sara Townsend
Series editor – Catherine Blake
Design – Katy Platt
Maps – Richard Hale
Typesetting – Filmer Ltd
Repro – PDQ Digital Media Solutions
Printers – Printed in Italy by Printer Trento srl
Publisher – Filmer Ltd

Email – info@hg2.com
Website – www.hg2.com

First Published in the United Kingdom in December 2006 by
Filmer Ltd
47 Filmer Road,
London SW6 7JJ

ISBN – 1-905428-05-7 / 978-1-905428-05-2

Hg2 Paris

CONTENTS

How to...

A Hedonist's guide to... is broken down into easy to use sections:
Sleep, Eat, Drink, Snack, Party, Culture, Shop, Play and Info. In each of
these sections you will find detailed reviews and photographs. At the
front of the book you will find an introduction to the city and an
overview map, followed by introductions to the four main areas and
more detailed maps. On each of these maps you will see the places
that we have reviewed, laid out by section, highlighted on the map with
a symbol and a number. To find out about a particular place simply turn
to the relevant section, where all entries are listed alphabetically.
Alternatively, browse through a specific section (e.g. Eat) until you find
a restaurant that you like the look of. Next to your choice will be a
small coloured dot – each colour refers to a particular area of the city.
Simply turn to the relevant map to discover the location.

Updates

Hg2 have developed a network of journalists in each city to review the
best hotels, restaurants, bars, clubs, etc., and to keep track of the latest
developments – new places open up all the time, while others simply
fade away or just go out of style. To access our free updates as well as
the content of each guide, simply log onto our website www.Hg2.com
and register. We welcome your help. If you have any comments or
recommendations, please feel free to email us at info@hg2.com.

Book your hotel on Hg2.com

We believe that the key to a great city break is choosing the right
hotel. Our unique site now enables you to browse through our selection of hotels, using the interactive maps to give you a good feel for

the area as well as the nearby restaurants, bars, sights, etc., before you book. Hg2 has formed partnerships with the hotels featured in our guide to bring them to readers at the lowest possible price. Our site now incorporates special offers from selected hotels, as well as a diary of interesting events taking place, 'Inspire Me'.

The concept

A Hedonist's guide to… is designed to appeal to a more urbane and stylish traveller. The kind of traveller who is interested in gourmet food, elegant hotels and seriously chic bars – the traveller who feels the need to explore, shop and pamper themselves away from the crowds.

Our aim is to give you an insider's knowledge of a city, to make you feel like a well-heeled, sophisticated local and to take you to the most fashionable places in town to rub shoulders with the local glitterati.

In today's world work rules our life, and weekends away are few and far between; when we do manage to get away we want to have as much fun and to relax as much as possible with the minimum amount of stress. This guide is all about maximizing time. There is a photograph of each place we feature, so before you go you know exactly what you are getting into; choose a restaurant or bar that suits you and your needs.

We pride ourselves on our independence and our integrity. We eat in all the restaurants, drink in all the bars and go wild in the nightclubs – all totally incognito. We charge no one for the privilege for appearing in the guide, and every place is reviewed and included at our discretion.

We feel cities are best enjoyed by soaking up the atmosphere: wander the streets, indulge in some retail therapy, re-energize yourself with a massage and then get ready to eat like a king and party hard on the local scene.

Paris

Ah, Gay Paris, city of lights, city of love. Capital of fashion and food. Its name alone raises the spirits of luminaries from Rimbaud to Robespierre, from Picasso to the Scarlet Pimpernel. We associate it with the technicolour magic of Gigi and macaroons, with a dancing Gene Kelly singing Gershwin tunes, with the risqué can-can dance of the Moulin Rouge, with gastronomic indulgence and sumptuous shops, with champagne cocktails … in short, with hedonism.

But Paris has a much darker side, having witnessed some of the blood-iest episodes of modern history from the Revolution through to the Occupation. It is also a city of contradictions and surprises: Paris is perceived to be small, but is in fact the most densely populated area in the western world outside Manhattan. It is known for being low-rise and yet contains what was the tallest building in the world for the first 30 years of the 20th century.

Paris began as the Roman settlement of Lutetia in around 50ad and by around 500ad had risen to be the capital of the Frankish empire. After a lull in its influence the city again became the capital of France after the Hundred Years War, although the kings of France generally pre-ferred to hold court away from the urban mob, first in the chateaux of the Loire valley and later at the famous Palace of Versailles. And with good reason, as the 14 July 1789 saw the defining moment of the city's history in the storming of the Bastille and the start of the Revolution.

After the chaos that ensued, the period of terror and the violence and glory of the Napoleonic period, Paris began to take the shape we are familiar with today under the auspices of Emperor Napoleon III and Baron Hausmann. Huge areas of medieval slums were cleared to make way for grand avenues and extravagant neo-classical monuments. If you have not already been to Paris to see them, you will have almost certainly seen them on the canvases of the Impressionists, who encapsulated the spirit of la belle-époque and its wonderfully sexy demi-monde. Even the Nazis succumbed to Paris' charm. General Choltitz refused Hitler's order to leave the city in ruins at the end of the Occupation in 1944, preserving it for posterity.

Today, Paris is a diverse and multi-faceted metropolis. It revels in its place as a home to almost every significant artistic and intellectual movement that Europe has seen in modern times. But with such a privileged cultural position come problems of its own and socio-economic inequalities that have brought unrest in its place, from the student demonstrations in the 1960s, to the race-related riots of 2005.

However, their unique variant of national pride resists the dilution of culture, so unlike England and America, Paris hasn't yet been overtaken by global chains.

Paris is the city of the flâneur and its compact size is ideal for roaming. It's just as important to while away the hours shopping or watching the world go by from a sun-soaked terrace with a café crème or aper-itif, as it is to visit the Louvre.

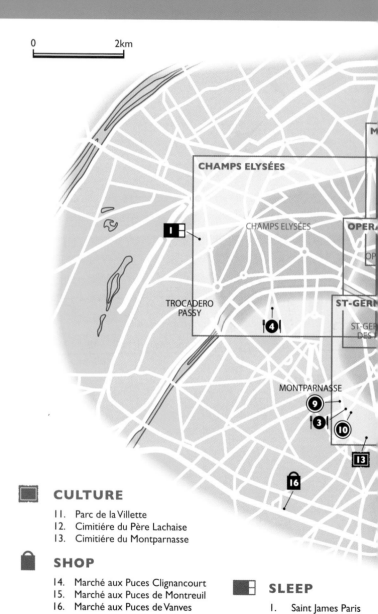

0   **2km**

CHAMPS ELYSÉES

CHAMPS ELYSÉES

OPERA

OP

TROCADERO
PASSY

ST-GER

ST-GER
DES

4

MONTPARNASSE

9

3   **10**

13

16

CULTURE

11. Parc de la Villette
12. Cimitiére du Père Lachaise
13. Cimitiére du Montparnasse

SHOP

14. Marché aux Puces Clignancourt
15. Marché aux Puces de Montreuil
16. Marché aux Puces de Vanves

SLEEP

1. Saint James Paris

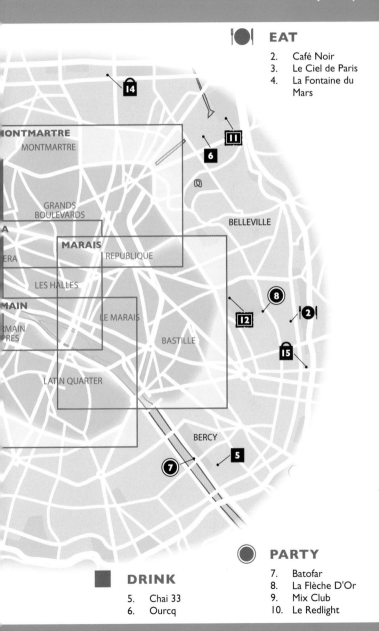

Paris city map

EAT

2. Café Noir
3. Le Ciel de Paris
4. La Fontaine du Mars

MONTMARTRE
MONTMARTRE

GRANDS
BOULEVARDS

BELLEVILLE

A

MARAIS
REPUBLIQUE

ERA

LES HALLES

RMAIN

LE MARAIS

RMAIN
PRES

BASTILLE

LATIN QUARTER

BERCY

DRINK

5. Chai 33
6. Ourcq

PARTY

7. Batofar
8. La Flèche D'Or
9. Mix Club
10. Le Redlight

Louvre & Palais Royal

It's no coincidence that the numbering of the Parisian arrondissements begins here: the Louvre, the Tuileries and Palais Royal form the geographical and royal heart of Paris, while the Seine runs through the city like its life blood. One cannot wander around this area without thinking of France's past monarchy. Stroll through the formal Tuileries gardens, loved by Monet and Renoir, and picture the Royal Palace, burnt down by Communists in 1871, where Louis XVI and Marie-Antoinette were kept under house arrest.

Today, a summer pleasure fair and Ferris wheel, offering the most outstanding views of Paris as well as the soaring sense of touching the sky, have replaced the angry mobs of the Revolution. Another sight worth catching on the way to the Louvre is through the Arc du Carrousel, which frames a view of the Concorde obelisk, the Arc de Triomphe and La Défence in almost perfect alignment.

The Louvre began life as a royal palace in the 13th century, and served as a power base right up to the German Occupation, when its rooms were used as offices. It is also a symbol of power: President Mitterand used it as an opportunity to reaffirm his presidential legacy by commissioning I.M. Pei to build the glass pyramid entrance. The Louvre houses the world's largest art collection, where crowds of culture-vultures, tourists and now Da Vinci coders flock. They take their sightseeing breaks sitting on the edge of the water features surrounding the pyramid, under the watchful eyes of flâneurs sipping Kir Royals at Le Café Marly on the Cour Napoleon du Louvre.

The Palais Royal opposite is an arcaded retreat, where the area's past residents, including Colette and Jean Cocteau, Napoleon and Victor Hugo, dined at Le Grand Véfour, one of the oldest restaurants in Paris. Alongside the restaurant you'll find boutiques offering, among other things, vintage fashion and military medals, as well as parfumeur Serge

Lutens' first shop. Behind the Palais Royal is the wonderfully old-fashioned shopping arcade Galerie Vivienne and the Bibliothèque Nationale Richelieu, where noteworthy contemporary photography exhibitions take place.

Napoleon crops up again, this time in the form of a bronze statue at the centre of the place Vendôme, which is rather apt as this square quietly exudes snobbishness and self-importance. It is home to the Ritz and *haute-joaillerie* names such as Cartier and Boucheron. Follow on from here down the shop-lined rue de la Paix to see Charles Garnier's magnificent neo-baroque opera house, perhaps stopping off at the tourist hot-spot Café de la Paix, if you fancy it.

At the other end of avenue de l'Opéra, crossing right through the 1st arrondissement, is rue du Saint-Honoré, a continuation of the luxurious shopping stretch of the rue du Faubourg-St-Honoré in the 8th, and of equal shopping interest. Concept store Colette, at no. 213, is a must for any fashion slave.

Les Halles, the 19th-century food market, was torn down in 1969 to make way for the huge and monstrous shopping complex, Forum des Halles, now terrorized by kids from 'les banlieues' who come to roam the teen-spirit shops of the vicinity (the Forum is a major RER-métro station connecting the suburbs to the city). Until mayor Bertrand Delanoë fulfils his promise to regenerate the site, avoid it.

However, rue de Montorgueil is pleasant place for a stroll, and is home to one of Paris' most exclusive spas (Nuxe, at no. 32). It crosses over rue Etienne Marcel, which, along with parallel rue Tiquetonne, is home to young street wear shops such as Diesel.

Both streets take you to rue Montmartre, which is home, along with its side streets, to many vibrant bars (Somo seems to have past its sell-by date, but Café Noir and Dédé la Frite are always busy). To the west is the Bourse, Paris' Stock Exchange. Continue northwards and you will hit the Grands Boulevards that line the border to the 9th arrondissement.

EAT

10. Apicius
11. La Cantine du Faubourg
12. Le Cristal Room
13. Maison Blanche
14. Market
15. Mood
16. Pavillon Ledoyen
17. Pershing Hall
18. Sens
19. Tokyo Eat

 PARTY

27. Le Baron
28. Man de la Ray
29. Queen

 CULTURE

30. Eiffel Tower
31. Palais de Tokyo

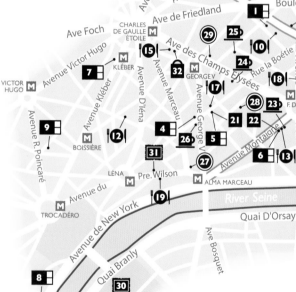

Louvre & Palais Royal local map

SHOP

- ◼ Faubourg-Saint-Honoré
- ◼ Avenue Montaigne
- 32. Drugstore Publicis

M Metro Station

0   500m

SNACK

- 23. La Galerie des Gobelins
- 24. Ladurée
- 25. Lô Sushi
- 26. Renoma Café Gallery

DRINK

- 20. Café Chic
- 21. Lounge Bar
- 22. The Bar

SLEEP

- 1. Le A
- 2. Le Bristol
- 3. Le Faubourg
- 4. L'Hôtel De Sers
- 5. Pershing Hall
- 6. Plaza Athénée
- 7. Raphael
- 8. Sezz
- 9. Trocadéro Dokan's

Champs-Élysées & Trocadéro

The 16th arrondissement – known as the Chaillot Quarter – was formally the village of Chaillot, which was absorbed into Paris in the 19th century, and architecturally transformed by Haussmann into the grand avenues and opulent mansions it is today. Many are now embassies, but it still remains Paris' most exclusive residential area.

Directly in front of the Eiffel Tower across the Seine is the Jardin Trocadéro, its fountains beautifully lit at night, where crowds congregate to watch the fireworks, the highlight of the 14 July celebrations. Underneath the Jardin Trocadéro is the recently reopened aquarium alongside 'CineAqua', a showcase for animation, and the unique Japanese restaurant Ozu, where you can watch the piscine habitats while eating… raw fish!

The Place du Trocadéro was built for the 1878 Universal Exhibition along with the Palais de Trocadéro. The Palais was demolished to make way for the new Palais de Chaillot, a curved, winged building, built for the World Fair of 1937 – a fusion of neo-classical architecture and Art Deco – which is home to four museums and a theatre.

From here, the avenue President Wilson – which has Paris' largest concentration of museums – leads you to the funky Palais de Tokyo, which combines contemporary art, 'fooding' and shopping in one stripped-down warehouse space. The Galliera opposite is Paris' fashion museum, housing over 100,000 outfits from the 18th century to the present day… but if you'd rather buy than simply look, then the adjoining arrondissement of the 8th is shopping central (for the posh shops, at least).

Probably the most famous shopping stretch in Paris is the avenue des Les Champs-Élysées. Though heavily commercialized, it is still the chicest 'high-street' in the world, with its wide pavements and cafés, chestnut trees and bordered flowerbeds that turn into larger green spaces towards the place de la Concorde. Within the greenery sit the new additions to Paris' already long list of art galleries, the 'Grand' and the 'Petit' Palais, both built for the Universal Exhibition of 1900, as was the incredibly ornate rococo Alexandre III bridge, which, with its nymphs and cherubs, is super-kitsch.

Following years of neglect, both the 'Grand' and the 'Petit' Palais have been renovated over the last decade. The 'Grand' holds temporary exhibitions (it's also where the Germans kept their tanks) and is worth visiting just to see the magnificent glass cupola, ironwork and glass Art Nouveau roof. The Petit now houses the Musée des Beaux-arts de la Ville de Paris, the place to go if you like Ingres, Delacroix and Courbet. Your transition from the 16th to the 8th doesn't alter the level of swank: you enter the 'golden triangle', and you drool at the shop windows of the swish rue Faubourg-Saint-Honoré. Don't wear anything but haute-designer – it's important to look the part when stopping off for extortionate cocktails at any of the area's exclusive hotel bars.

CULTURE

PLAY

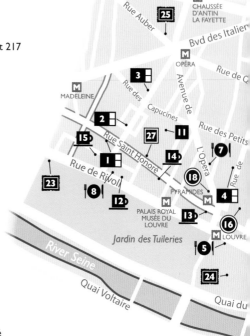

SHOP

EAT

DRINK

SLEEP

Champs-Élysées & Trocadéro local map

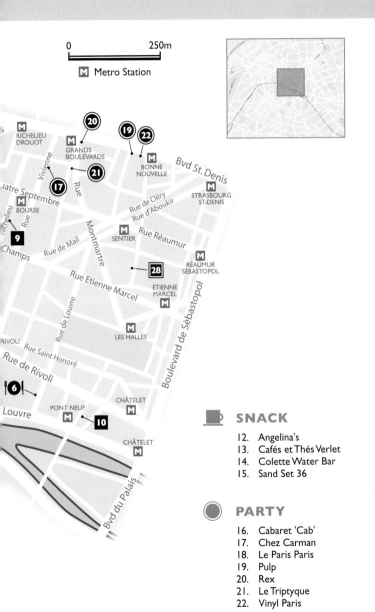

0   250m

M Metro Station

RICHELIEU DROUOT

GRANDS BOULEVARDS

Bvd St. Denis

BONNE NOUVELLE

STRASBOURG ST-DENIS

Vivienne

Rue

Quatre Septembre

BOURSE

Richelieu

Rue

Rue de Cléry

Rue d'Aboukir

Rue Réaumur

9

Champs

Rue de Mail

Montmartre

SENTIER

RÉAUMUR SÉBASTOPOL

28

Rue Etienne Marcel

ÉTIENNE MARCEL

Boulevard de Sébastopol

Louvre

Rue de Louvre

LES HALLES

RIVOLI

Rue Saint Honoré

Rue de Rivoli

6

Louvre

PONT NEUF

10

CHÂTELET

CHÂTELET

Bvd du Palais

☕ SNACK

12. Angelina's
13. Cafés et Thés Verlet
14. Colette Water Bar
15. Sand Set 36

● PARTY

16. Cabaret 'Cab'
17. Chez Carman
18. Le Paris Paris
19. Pulp
20. Rex
21. Le Triptyque
22. Vinyl Paris

The Left Bank & Latin Quarter

The Left Bank probably sums up our romantic vision of Paris as epitomized by musicals such as *Gigi* and An *American in Paris*. Home to the Sorbonne, École des Beaux-Arts and University Paris-Jussieu, and lined with booksellers – including Shakespeare & Co. at 37 rue de la Bûcherie – the area is filled with students populating a vibrant café scene, while the hard-hitting Lefties of the 1968 student riots have gone (it was also popular with Resistance fighters). The nightlife centres on debates over cheeseboards in wine bars, as trendier nightspots have relocated to the old working-class districts of the Rive Droite.

The Left Bank feels touristy, but is also incredibly chic: a range of smart boutiques cater for the grown-up intelligensia, who, having graduated from the Sorbonne, remained in the locale. Those who found work in publishing houses around the cobbled streets of Saint-Andre-des-Arts perpetuate the atmosphere of existentialist enquiry begun by Sartre, de Beauvoir and Camus in Les Deux Magots and Café Flore. Incidentally, Saint-Germain gets its name from Paris' oldest church.

The skyline of the Left Bank is dominated by the Tour Montparnasse, Europe's second tallest tower; the Montparnasse area, adopted by George Sand and Chopin in the mid-1800s, was popular in the early 20th century with Trotsky and Lenin, and then the 1920s and 1930s with Picasso, Hemingway, Cocteau and Matisse – all of whom hung out in local bars discussing modern revolutions in politics and art. The fully restored 1880s décor of the wonderful Théâtre Montparnasse is a must: have a drink in the run-down yet atmospheric bar downstairs. If you're in need of some green space, stroll along the tree-lined boulevard Edgar Quinet nearby, where an art market has established itself. Otherwise the Jardin du Luxembourg offers neat gravelled paths through manicured gardens.

Latin was the language of the scholars of the 13th–century university La Sorbonne – hence the name 'Quartier Latin' (Latin Quarter). It is the location of the Panthéon, an impressively large church that now only acts as a monumental crypt, encasing the remains of great French men and one woman, including Voltaire, Zola, Dumas and Marie Curie.

There is a village-like daily market on rue Mouffetard, which leads off the picturesque place de la Contrescarpe; although very pleasant to stroll through by day, the area becomes rather tacky at night, marred by a continuous stretch of tourist-filled restaurants. Worthwhile sites in the Latin Quarter include the Jardin des Plantes, a garden and zoo with a fin-de-siècle natural history museum featuring taxidermy, with 1930s greenhouses attached; the Institut du Monde Arabe, with its noteworthy architecture by Jean Nouvel and its roof-top restaurant; and La Mosquée de Paris, with its atmospheric dining and tea room, as well as a hammam (Turkish steam baths).

The French Parliament, L'Assemblée Nationale, dominates the rather sedate 7th arrondissement. Unless you want to visit the UNESCO headquarters or the prime minister's official residence, there is no real reason to come here – civil service offices, embassies and ministries, guarded by bored gendarmes, take up long stretches. However, the high-end fashion and design shops near the border of the 6th should not be ignored.

The 7th is only referred to in guide books as Les Invalides, because the great Hôtel des Invalides is its prime tourist destination, along with the Musée d'Orsay, Musée Rodin and Tour Eiffel. Built by Louis XIV as a hospital for his wounded and homeless soldiers, it has a golden-domed church at the back – the Eglise du Dôme – which houses the remains of Napoleon Bonaparte in its crypt. The 18th-century buildings of the École Militaire, along with the Parc du Champs de Mars, stretch down to the Eiffel Tower and come to life with fireworks and crowds on 14 July.

⬤ PARTY

38. Le Cameleon Jazz Club
39. Wagg

0   500m

Ⓜ Metro Station

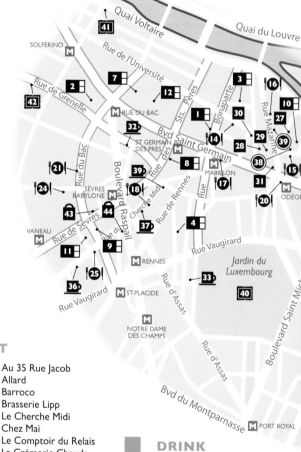

▮◯▮ EAT

14. Au 35 Rue Jacob
15. Allard
16. Barroco
17. Brasserie Lipp
18. Le Cherche Midi
19. Chez Mai
20. Le Comptoir du Relais
21. La Crémerie Chaude
22. La Mosquée de Paris
23. My Room:
24. Au Pied de Fouet
25. Le Rousseau
26. Ziryab

▮ DRINK

27. L'Assignat
28. Le Bar du Marché
29. Les Etages
30. La Palette
31. Le Pub Saint-Germain

The Left Bank & Latin Quarter local map

SLEEP

1. Bel Ami
2. Duc de Saint-Simon
3. L'Hôtel
4. Hôtel de L'Abbaye
5. Hôtel Grandes Écoles
6. Hôtel des Grands Hommes
7. Hôtel Montalembert
8. Hôtel des Saint-Pères
9. Le Placide
10. Relais Christine
11. Saint-Grégoire
12. Saint Thomas D'Aquin
13. Villa d'Estrées

SNACK

32. Café Le Basile
33. Café Fleurus
34. Le Confiturier
35. La Contrescarpe
36. Mamie Gateaux
37. Poilâne

13
ST MICHEL Ⓜ
CLUNY
LA SORBONNE Ⓜ
Quai de la Tournelle
19
Bvd Saint Germain
Ⓜ MAUBERT MUTUALITÉ
Rue Saint Jacques
Rue des Ecoles
6
23
LUXEMBOURG
Rue Clovis
Rue Monge
Ⓜ CARDINAL LEMOINE
Ⓜ JUSSIEU
Bvd Henri IV
26
Quai Saint Bernard
River Seine
Rue Cuvier
Jardin des Plantes
Gay - Lussac
35
5
Rue Mouffetard
Ⓜ PLACE MONGE
Rue Monge
22
Rue Claude Bernard
Ⓜ CENSIER DAUBENTON

SHOP

▪ Boulevard Saint Germain
▪ Rue Bonaparte
▪ Rue du Bac
▪ Rue de Grenelle
▪ Rue des Saints Pères
43. Bon Marché Rive Gauche
44. Marché Raspail

CULTURE

40. Jardin du Luxembourg
41. Musée d'Orsay
42. Musée Rodin

Marais, Bastille & Oberkampf

The Colonne de Juillet is a column – upholding the golden, winged figure representing the 'Spirit of Liberty' – commemorating the uprising of 1830. It stands on the former site of the Bastille prison, stormed by angry mobs demanding freedom from the feudal state and precipitating the start of the 1789 French Revolution. But the giant, imposing glass building of the Opéra Bastille, which formed part of Mitterrand's 'grands travaux', overshadows it.

This is traditionally the furniture-makers' district, but these artisans are swiftly disappearing to be replaced by trendy street-wear shops and bars. The streets immediately surrounding the Opéra and column are congested and polluted, and feel like a thoroughfare – not the most salubrious place to be sipping a coffee on the pavement. Better bars and cafés are to be found just behind the Bastille, away from the grime of the traffic. Rue Charenton has the ever-cool restaurant-cum-bar the China Club, and around the corner is the vibrant North African market square of place d'Aligre and its surrounding wine bars. Don't forget, either, the rue de Charonne where the long-established Pause Café still manages  to draw in a cool crowd. Having said that, Bastille has not managed to retain the exclusively cool status it achieved in the 1990s: its hipness, although still present, has been diluted by the presence of more commercial ventures.

Rue Oberkampf, on the other hand, has now attained such heights of popularity that the area it dominates, between boulevard Voltaire and boulevard Ménilmontant and Belleville, is collectively referred to as 'Oberkampf'. This rise has been attributed to the rediscovery of Café Charbon on rue Oberkampf itself, which first opened at the turn of the century but was revolutionized by a trendy crowd about 15 years ago. A club has now opened next door, and the prevalence of fantastic nightlife has spread to rue Saint-Maur and rue Jean Pierre Timbaud.

The area south of Bastille, towards Gare de Lyon, has been the subject of regeneration projects, such as the Viaduc des Arts belonging to the former Paris-Vincennes railway line along Avenue Daumesnil. The old railway lines above the viaduct have been landscaped into a green park walkway – a 'planted promenade'. The red-brick arches and space underneath have been scrubbed and cleaned to the point of sterilization, to make room for the row of retail outlets, including antique shops and galleries, which have become rather soulless, overpriced and disappointing. The Bercy Village, known as Cour Saint-Emilion, is a lot better, and although it is reminiscent of a Club Med in terms of its artificiality, it has an excellent wine bar, Chai 33. The new Bibliothèque Nationale opposite, just across the Seine, was commissioned by François Mitterrand to look like four upstanding books and is impressive, especially at night.

EAT

8. 404
9. Anahi
10. Le Chateaubriand
11. Chez Marianne
12. Curieux Spaghetti Bar
13. Les Fous de L'île
14. Georges
15. L'Homme Bleu
16. Kodo
17. Le Murano
18. Le Petit Marché
19. Le Réfectoire
20. Le Taxi Jaune
21. Le Train Bleu

SHOP

- Rue Charlot
- Rue des Francs Bourgeois
- Rue Vieille-du-Temple
- Rue des Rosiers
60. Rue Ferdinand Duval
61. Rue Poitou
62. Rue St. Croix de la Bretonnerie

SLEEP

1. Bourg Tibourg
2. Caron de Beaumarchais
3. Duo
4. Hôtel du Jeu de Paume
5. Hôtel du Petit Moulin
6. Murano Urban Resort
7. Pavillon de la Reine

CULTURE

52. Cirque d'Hiver Bouglione
53. Le Jeu de Paume
54. Maison Européene de la Photographie
55. La Maison Rouge
56. Mémorial des Martyrs de la Déportation
57. Musée National Picasso
58. Music at Chatelet
59. Opéra de la Bastille

PLAY

63. Les Bains du Marais
64. Nickel

RÉAUMUR SÉBASTOPOL
RÉPUBLIQUE
Rue du Faub
TEMPLE
Rue de Turbigo
Boulevard
ARTS ET MÉTIERS
Ave
Boulevard de Sébastopol
Rue Saint Martin
Rue Beaubourg
Rue du Temple
Bvd du Temple
OBERK
FILLES DU CALVAIRE
RAMBUTEAU
Rue de Turenne
ST SÉBASTIEN FROISSART
Rue Beaumarchais
Rue de Rivoli
HOTEL-DE-VILLE
Rue des Francs Bourgeois
Boulevard Richard
ST PAUL
Rue St. Antoine
Q. de l'Hôtel de Ville
PONT-MARIE
BASTILLE
Boulevard Beaumarchais
Bvd Henri IV
SULLY-MORLAND
Quai Henri IV
Bvd Bourbon
Bvd de la Bastille
Rue de Lyon
Quai Saint Bernard
River Seine
QUAI DE LA RAPEE
Bvd D
Avenue

Marais, Bastille & Oberkampf local map

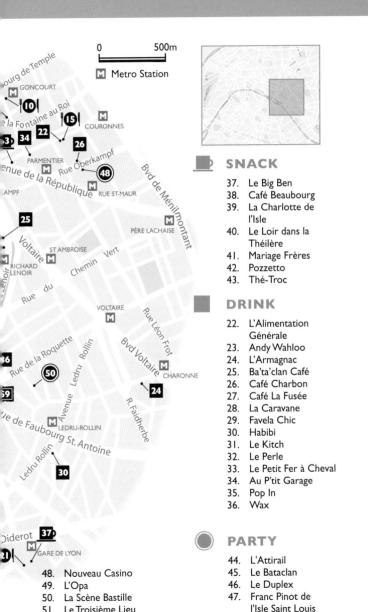

0   500m

M Metro Station

SNACK

37. Le Big Ben
38. Café Beaubourg
39. La Charlotte de l'Isle
40. Le Loir dans la Théilère
41. Mariage Frères
42. Pozzetto
43. Thé-Troc

DRINK

22. L'Alimentation Générale
23. Andy Wahloo
24. L'Armagnac
25. Ba'ta'clan Café
26. Café Charbon
27. Café La Fusée
28. La Caravane
29. Favela Chic
30. Habibi
31. Le Kitch
32. Le Perle
33. Le Petit Fer à Cheval
34. Au P'tit Garage
35. Pop In
36. Wax

PARTY

44. L'Attirail
45. Le Bataclan
46. Le Duplex
47. Franc Pinot de l'Isle Saint Louis

48. Nouveau Casino
49. L'Opa
50. La Scène Bastille
51. Le Troisième Lieu

Montmartre

Anyone who is familiar with the paintings of the Impressionists will recognize Les Grands Boulevards, which epitomize the urban regeneration of the Second Empire overseen by Haussmann. Dominated by the *grands magasins* (department stores) at one end, the boulevards continue through to place de la République, another Haussmann creation symbolizing the Republic of 1883, and onto the Bastille, changing names six times. Northwards, into the 9th and 18th arrondissement, is the area known as Montmartre.

The best stretch is the rue des Martyrs. Make sure you sample an award-winning croissant from the Boulangerie Arnaud Delmontel, eat at the coolest hotel in Paris – Hôtel Amour – on rue Navarin, and stroll down the tree-lined avenue Trudaine alongside the boho-chic locals.

Sacré-Coeur stands on top of a hill known as La Butte (the 'mound'). The closer you get to it, the more the streets seem to be dominated by cheap-looking crêpe stalls and souvenir shops, but the unbearable hordes of tourists are the worst. It was once famous for being a hub of creativity – Van Gogh, Renoir, Picasso and Braque to name but a few had their studios here – but unfortunately the only artistic legacy remaining is the portrait artists who cackle for your custom. It's best to stay at the bottom of La Butte, around the bohemian area of the place des Abbesses, where you'll find many quirky shops and designer ateliers. These streets were designed for aimless wandering (and strong calf muscles). Look out for the trendy café Burq on rue Burq, and on the winding rue Lepic you'll find the Café des Deux Moulins at No. 15 (where the fictional Amélie Poulin of the cult film worked as a waitress), and Chez Camille on rue Ravignan, which is THE cool place to have a drink or coffee.

Pigalle, which is between these two areas, is the notorious red-light district, where tourist dance-halls such as the Moulin Rouge sit next to more gritty brothel bars and X-rated video shops.

It was President Pompidou's wish to tarmac the Canal Saint-Martin and make way for a motorway, but thank goodness he did not get his way – the city would have forever lost one of its most enchanting areas. Originally created by Napoleon in the early 19th century to give Parisians drinking water, the canal later became an invaluable asset for the rising industries of the later part of the century. Today, the barges are a less frequent sight. The footbridges and cobbled canalside has become a popular picnic spot, and there are many wonderful shabby–chic restaurants and bars waiting to be discovered. The area has been gentrified in recent years – shops such as Agnès b. have sprung up – but many of the original independents still remain, along with one of the city's best art bookshops, Artazart. Across the canal to the east is Belleville, a more run-down working-class area, caricatured in the Oscar-winning animation. Behind the immense Saint-Louis hospital are bar-filled streets, in particular the dilapidated rue Sainte-Marthe leading to place Saint-Marthe, unparalleled in bohemian atmosphere.

Continue up the canal, past the Rotonde de la Ville to the quais of the Seine and Loire, where you will find the stylish MK2 cinema complex and restaurant. Still further on lies the entertainment and cultural city of Parc de la Villette.

The rather scruffy rue du Faubourg-Saint-Denis that cuts right through the 10th arrondissement is home to the Indian community: although Passage Brady is atmospheric, the really authentic and now rather trendy Indian area is further up towards the Gare du Nord. Rue Cail and rue Louis-Blanc leading towards the canal are the places to go for a fantastic curry.

PLAY

31. Hammam des Grands Boulevards
32. UMA: Massage & Yoga

CULTURE

24. Le Grand Rex Cinema
25. Musée National Gustave-Moreau
26. Studio 28

EAT

4. Hôtel du Nord
5. Mme Shawn
6. Rôtisserie Sainte-Marthe
7. Le Sainte Marthe
8. Le Sporting

SLEEP

1. Amour
2. Kube
3. Villa Royale

PARTY

20. Le Divan du Monde
21. Folie's Pigalle
22. Glaz`art
23. Point Éphémère

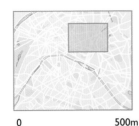

0   500m

M Metro Station

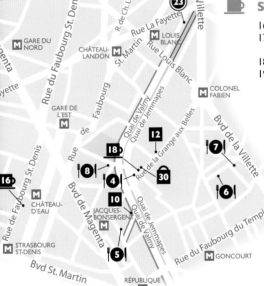

SNACK

16. Chez Jeannette
17. Aux Pipalottes Gourmandes
18. Pink Flamingo
19. Rose Bakery

SHOP

- Quai de Valmy
- Rue Beaurepaire
27. Galeries Lafayette
28. Printemps
29. Passage Jouffroy
30. Viveka Bergstorm

DRINK

9. Le Brébant
10. Chez Prune
11. De la Ville Café
12. La Fontaine
13. La Fourmi
14. Ice Kube
15. Le Rendezvous des Amis

sleep...

No. There is no shortage of hotels in Paris, possibly because it is the most visited city in the world. Accommodation ranges from the gigantic Hilton to the smaller independent hotel half-hidden by ivy on a cobblestone street, via the concept boutique hotels where you go to look and be seen.

There are the palatial hotels of the 'golden triangle' (such as the George V and Hôtel Plaza Athénée), and those in or around the place Vendôme (the Ritz). Of these, the Crillon must be the most spectacular, taking the chintzy gold leaf and marble look to vertiginous new heights. Then there are the wonderfully preserved hotels of old, run by the same family for almost a hundred years (the Raphael), as well as the traditional hotels that have been given a contemporary make-over (the Sers). And there are quirky one-offs with eccentric proprietors (Hôtel Caron de Beaumarchais), or the intimate, hidden treasures of the Left Bank, filled to the brim with character and antiques (Hôtel de L'Abbaye, Duc de Saint-Simon, Grandes Écoles).

Most hotels are steeped in history. You can live beyond your means, as Oscar Wilde did at L'Hôtel, drink like Hemingway in his eponymous bar at the Ritz or indulge in some abstract musing in the Hotel des Grands Hommes, where André Breton wrote his Surrealist Manifesto. You can rest your head in what used to be a 13th-century cloister at the Relais Christine or in a former World War II general's HQ at Pershing Hall, or even have your breakfast in a 15th-century tennis court at Hôtel du Jeu de Paume.

In recent years Paris has witnessed a surge in designer boutique hotels of every style and mood, from Jacques Garcia's opulent Napoleonic-boudoir interiors of the Bourg-Tibourg in the heart of the Marais and the Hôtel Costes on the exclusive shopping street of Saint-Honoré, to the pure bordello style of Villa Royale in the red-light district of Pigalle. There is minimalism to be found in Bel Ami in the literary Saint-Germain-des-Prés and places in which to fulfil rock-star fantasies, such as Kube near the Gare du Nord.

If it hasn't been designed by Garcia, Méchiche or Putman, it is likely to have been by one of their protégés, and Parisians are continuing to push the boundaries further with innovative concepts in hotel décor: haute couture's Christian Lacroix came up with the kooky look for the Hôtel du Petit Moulin, while Hôtel Amore sees hoteliers collaborating with club owners to commission contemporary artists such as Sophie Calle to decorate the rooms.

Parisians pride themselves on excellence of service, where the concierge becomes your personal butler. They comply to your every whim and fancy, best illustrated by the staff at the Hotel Meurice's granting Salvador Dali's request for a herd of sheep. Boutique hotels have replaced discreet gentleman concierges with well-heeled sassy ladies who behave more like your agent. Some have gone further at dispensing with the traditional formalities: the Sezz has scrapped the idea of a reception desk altogether.

Internet access, mini-bar and room service are standard, while many hotels now offer free WiFi and a direct telephone line too; and some will even compete for your custom with a complementary mini-bar (Pershing Hall). Most hotels charge breakfast as an extra, and although taking le petit-d at the Ritz or Plaza Athénée is the ultimate hedonist's start to the day (€80 approx.), it's a good reason to venture out and explore the many atmospheric street cafés Paris has to offer.

Be prepared to book well in advance, especially during the fashion weeks (first week in October, last week in January, last week in February, first week in March), and be warned that most boutique hotels are truly boutique in size.

Rates given are for a double room in low season to a suite in high season.

Our top 10 places to stay in Paris are:

1. Hôtel du Petit Moulin
2. L'Hôtel
3. Raphael
4. Pavillon de la Reine
5. Trocadéro Dokan's
6. Villa d'Estrées
7. Amour
8. Villa Royale
9. Le Placide
10. Murano Urban Resort

Our top 5 for style are:

1. Amour
2. Hôtel du Petit Moulin
3. Sezz
4. Murano Urban Resort
5. Pershing Hall

Our top 5 for atmosphere are:

1. Raphael
2. L'Hôtel
3. Hôtel des Grandes Écoles
4. Pavillon de la Reine
5. Villa Royale

Our top 5 for location are:

1. Pavillon de la Reine
2. Villa d'Estrées
3. The Ritz
4. Bourg Tibourg
5. Duo

Le A, 4 rue d'Artois, Champs-Élysées

Tel: 01 42 56 99 99 www.paris-hotel-a.com
Rates: €329–590

Boutique Hotel Le A is the marvellous result of the collaboration between interior-architect Frédéric Méchiche and artist Fabrice Hybert. Inside, the only colour to be seen is provided courtesy of Fabrice Hybert's wall-sized abstract paintings specifically commissioned for the space, while the rest of

the modern interior is purely black and white. Dark armchairs and sofas are accentuated with bright white cushions, while fabulous white orchids are reflected in the polished black coffee tables and echo the white painted brickwork that frames the angular modern fireplaces. The lobby is given added personality by the many tubular lights that are suspended at different heights. The bar/breakfast area is a celestial, South Beach fantasy: white drapes hang over the skylight, while large paintings of trees create the illusion of depth of space. The 25 rooms (and sole apartment) continue the black-and-white theme, providing a perfect backdrop to the colourful art and suspended lights. Impossibly white armchairs are a dry cleaner's fantasy, although you feel you only have to look at them to leave your mark. The black-and-white clad young designer guests graciously manage to echo the furniture, if only not to upset the décor.

Style 8, Atmosphere 8, Location 8

Amour, 8 rue de Navarin, Montmartre

Tel: 01 48 78 31 80 www.hotelamour.com
Rates: €150–200

Paris 2006: the calligraphic stencil of the word 'Amour' is seen everywhere on the pavements. A graffiti artist in love? Or a tag heralding the new Hotel Amour? The trendiest duo in Paris (owners of clubs Le Baron and Le Paris, Paris; see Party) have teamed up with one of the Costes boys (of Georges

at the Pompidou; see Eat) to create this hotel and restaurant. Each of the 20 rooms has its own style and character, which is so defined that one could give them themed titles. 'Playboy bachelor pad': a million magazines and books of 1970s female models surround the all-black walls, sheets and carpet. 'Teenage boy's room': a skateboard casually leans by the bed with robot toys everywhere. Artists and illustrators have been given free rein with the décor in other rooms. Kiehl's products fill the bathrooms. Japanese chocolate biscuits wait on the bed. A pink, rather overexcited and adult-rated Mickey Mouse guards the reception desk, behind which pretty things (none of whom could be a day older than 25) seem to be 'playing at hotel'. The restaurant is joyously simple: bright red banquettes, Danish chairs and a beautiful garden for the warmer months. Quite possibly the coolest hotel in Paris.

Style 8/9, Atmosphere 8, Location 8

Bel Ami, 7–11 rue Saint-Benoît, Saint-Germain
Tel: 01 42 61 53 53 www.hotel-bel-ami.com
Rates: €270–520

The hotel Bel Ami takes its name from Guy de Maupassant's eponymous novel in an attempt to draw on the literary heritage of the Saint-Germain area, but there is little else about this Zen-style establishment that reflects it. The elegant minimalism of the interior is designed to exude calm and tranquillity, with the whole possessing a delicate smell of green tea. When it first opened in 2000 it caused a bit of a stir, but has since been overshadowed by other designer hotels in Paris. In response to the competition, Bel Ami has opened a new spa, which includes three exclusive treatment rooms and a gym complete with fish tank and large flat-screen TV. The opening of a

café seems less wise, especially with Café Flore and Les Deux Magots around the corner. Rooms come in three shades – green, blue and orange ('one to suit each mood') – perhaps trying too hard to please all and therefore lacking in impact.

Style 8, Atmosphere 6, Location 8

Bourg Tibourg, 19 rue du Bourg Tibourg, Marais
Tel: 01 42 78 47 39 www.hotelbourgtibourg.com
Rates: €160–350

Legendary designer Jacques Garcia, who has decorated numerous boutique hotels in Paris (Costes, L'Hôtel and Villa d'Estrées to name but three), has here blended Orientalism with a touch of Victoriana and a bit of Gothic. Tasselled lampshades, opulent striped drapes, silky fringes and dark wood furniture decorate all of the communal areas and 31 rooms. The narrow passageways and dimly lit stairwells, with their kaleidoscope of colours and textures, conjure up the atmosphere of a Belle Époque luxury whorehouse.

It belongs to the Costes mafia, so part of the romantic trimming is the good-looking and slightly snooty staff, as well as all the necessary mod-cons. Its location is perfect, right in the heart of the Marais, and it occupies the same street as the fabulous teahouse Mariage Frères (see Snack) and delicious restaurant Kodo (see Eat). But there is a sacrifice to be made, and that is space: the hotel is tiny, with the smallest bathrooms and lift in Paris.

Style 8, Atmosphere 8, Location 9

Le Bristol, 112 rue du Faubourg-Saint-Honore, Champs-Élysées
Tel: 01 53 43 43 00 www.lebristol.com
Rates: €690–1,300

Change is in the air for Le Bristol: a new brand identity in funky lime-green and an impressive extension in a more modern décor. The newly revamped bar (open to 2am), decorated in warm amber tones, holds fashion shows every Saturday to coincide with afternoon tea. Otherwise, the hotel remains very traditional: white marble floors, Île-de-France stone walls and gilded glass cabinets advertising classic perfumes and Cartier watches, which are dotted around the pink-marbled columns of the chandelier-lined lobby. The Jewish architect Lerman designed the metal grillework of the fabulous old

lift when he was hiding here during World War II, his room number having been erased from the hotel register. There are 162 rooms, including 73 grand suites, all decorated in a classic style: antique furniture, rare wood panelling, fine European fabrics and timeless paintings. The hotel boasts a two Michelin-starred summer and winter restaurant, a beautiful garden, and an Anne Sémonin Spa, as well as a rooftop swimming pool designed by naval architect Professor Pinnau, who built boats for Onassis. If you're brave enough to face the crazy Parisian drivers, a Smart car is available to guests (€10 for 3 hours).

Style 7, Atmosphere 8, Location 8

Caron de Beaumarchais, 12 rue Vieille-du-Temple, Marais
Tel: 01 42 72 34 12 www.carondebeaumarchais.com
Rates: €125–162

An antique card table left mid-game, lighted candles, a chair propped up on a pianoforte dating from 1792, an open sheet of music displayed on a music stand by an ornately carved wooden harp… Hotel Caron de Beaumarchais is like a cross between an 18th-century home, suddenly abandoned by its owners, and a carefully crafted stage-set: one half expects actors in period wigs and ball gowns to take up where the inhabitants left off. Framed collages, lovingly put together, of old manuscripts and etchings hang on the walls, which are decorated with only the best French wallpaper and curtain fabrics. Owner and former antique dealer, Alain Bigeard, takes his inspiration for all of this from the quartier's late resident, Caron de Beaumarchais, who was, among many things, an aristocrat, watchmaker to Louis XV and author of *The Marriage of Figaro* (hence the musical and literary theme). The antique look is continued in the wooden-beamed bedrooms, which are small (a Marais symptom) and unfortunately overpowered by

the smell of air freshener. It's a shame that Alain gave in to repeated requests for television sets, which sit rather incongruously with the décor. Nevertheless, the hotel is unique, and it's worth staying here for Alain's wealth of knowledge on the history of Paris alone.

Style 7, Atmosphere 8, Location 9

Costes, 239 rue St-Honoré

Tel: 01 42 44 50 00
Rates: €400–2,800

The famous Costes bros team, Gilbert and Jean-Louis, opened their four-star Hôtel Costes in 1995 after the success of their Café Beaubourg and Café Marly. At the time the formula was ground-breaking: a super-designed, sumptuous setting by renowned decorator Jacques Garcia, in an eclectic mix

of styles – from Napoleonic Second Empire to opulent boudoir (even the armchairs have tassels) – with a bar and restaurant that were intended to become (and certainly became) just as important and trendy as the hotel itself. Their commissioning of an in-house DJ, Stéphane Pompougnac, was probably what catapulted the hotel to make it stand out. Pompougnac's 'Costes' CDs have sold globally to great acclaim, pushing the brand internationally. It immediately became the place to see and be seen, stuffed with celebrities and beautiful people lounging about the courtyard and pool. Over 10 years later, however, the formula has become a little staid, having been reproduced by the Costes mafia themselves alongside many copycats. Garcia has since left his trademark décor on many other Parisian boutique hotels in which DJs have become as prerequisite as a mini-bar. Now the Costes has more celebrity spotters than true celebrities, yet the staff remain notoriously snooty, even by Parisian standards. More perplexing is the image the Hôtel Costes has of itself: while priding itself in being discrete, a hidden secret without a website, it's probably Paris' most talked about hotel. By selling its own merchandise at the reception desk for guests to show off at home, it transforms its image from classy chic to distasteful Disney. The rooms are brothel dark and seductive, whose with a balcony are the best. The hotel's notoriety will make it an unforgettable, if very expensive, stay whether you love it or hate it.

Style 9, Atmosphere 8, Location 9

Duc de Saint-Simon, 14 rue de Saint-Simon, Invalides
Tel: 01 44 39 20 20 www.hotelducdesaintsimon.com
Rates: €220–375

Tucked down a little side street in the boutique stretch of the 7th arrondissement, this 19th-century building with its old carriageway door, cobble-stoned courtyard (where guests enjoy their breakfasts in the summer months) and antique-filled interior is a true romantic hide-away. The faux marble, honey-coloured lobby may not be to everybody's taste (although the attention to detail is impressive – even the 'No smoking' sign has been hand painted), but it's difficult to resist the charm of the rest of the hotel. Here you will find austere oil paintings, Louis XVI velvet furnishings, fresh flower arrangements and a wonderful underground bar in the converted wine cellar. The 29 rooms are traditional in style and all a little

different – try to book one with a large private terrace. The current owner was so enthusiastic about the history of the place, which was converted into a hotel as far back as 1904, that he's produced a book about it: it's steeped in amusing anecdotes about misbehaving guests.

Style 8, Atmosphere 8, Location 8

Duo, 11, rue du Temple, Marais
Tel: 01 42 72 72 22 www.duoparis.com
Rates: €135–430

The Axial Beaubourg has been renovated and renamed Duo, so called for its two different styles of room (so make sure you get the receptionist to describe what you've booked on the telephone). Both are stylish, with flat-

screen TVs and all the mod-cons you could possibly need; but one has twin
beds pushed together, fuchsia bedcovers and headboards, violet-grey carpet
and walls, whilst the other has a double bed with leather headboard, two-
tone patterned wallpaper, and brown throws, carpet and curtains. The latter
is probably a touch trendier. Both are also a good size considering the hotel
is in the centre of the Marais. The communal areas are wonderfully spacious,
with oversized designer lampshades hanging from a wooden-beamed ceiling.
Fluffy rugs sit under tweed-upholstered armchairs, flat-screen TVs show off
video art, and large coffee tables are strewn with newspapers and magazines
for your enjoyment. Lovely.

Style 8, Atmosphere 8, Location 9

Le Faubourg, 15 rue Boissy d'Anglas, Louvre
Tel: 01 44 94 14 14 www.sofitelfaubourg.com
Rates: €375–2,500

Le Faubourg is tucked away between the Place de la Concorde and rue
Faubourg-Saint-Honoré, one of Paris' most exclusive shopping addresses.
The hotel takes the fashion industry as its theme, with original fashion illus-

trations by Jeanne Lanvin, one of the great couturiers of the early 20th century, along with classic black-and-white fashion photography, decorating its
walls. Japanese fashionistas dressed in black with funky haircuts and chunky
designer glasses mill about the lobby, alongside a clientele of elegant
Parisiennes of a certain age drinking coffee and discussing the latest edition
of *Vogue*. Architect Richard Martinet and designer Pierre Yves Rochon have

worked closely together to maintain the classic charm of the original building while adding functional features and more modern touches (updating classic furniture with contemporary fabrics, for example). The hallways are decorated with original drawings by Jules Chéret of Moulin Rouge/Belle Époque fame. The hotel's communal spaces – including the restaurant and bar – are worth visiting even if you're not staying there (see Eat and Drink). A favourite spot in the hotel, overlooking the main lobby, is a small library lined with lacquered ebony bookshelves and – for once – containing books you might actually want to read. It's a wonderful oasis of calm (if a celebrity interview isn't in progress) where you can enjoy a cocktail, and with its central fireplace it's super-cosy in the wintertime. Don't be put off by the fact that it's big – 173 rooms – as it is elegant, lovely and comfortable.

Style 8, Atmosphere 8, Location 8

L'Hôtel, 13 rue des Beaux-Arts, St Germain
Tel: 01 44 41 99 00 www.l-hotel.com
Rates: €255–640

Famed as the place where Oscar Wilde died, L'Hôtel is fittingly decadent. Appropriately situated in the literary district of the Left Bank, it has low ceilings, curtain drapes, ornate pictures and fireplaces, which offer a cosy yet luxurious stay. Each of the 20 rooms have been decorated according to a

theme: 'Marco Polo' is à la japonaise, with porcelain lamps and a pagoda-esque, wood-panelled bed; 'Mistinguett' (queen of the Paris music-hall) is all mirrored Art Deco (the bed actually used to belong to her); and 'Barroco' is all velvety red with dark bookcases and gold fittings. If you stay in the Oscar Wilde room, you can enjoy your own little private terrace and peacock mural, as well as various Oscar memorabilia. The hotel also has its own hammam down in its vaults, offering massages and thermal baths.

Style 9, Atmosphere 8, Location 8

Hôtel de l'Abbaye, 10 rue Cassette, St Germain
Tel: 01 45 44 38 11 www.hotel-abbaye.com
Rates: €205–472

Tucked away within a charming inner courtyard, down a quiet street in the heart of Saint-Germain-des-Prés, the Hotel de L'Abbaye has been run by the same independent owner since its opening in 1973. It's a mish-mash of design: the hallways have been furnished with black-and-red patterned carpets and timber squares on the walls, lending it a Japanese feel; three other rooms have a more masculine, contemporary look; while the remainder are typically ornate and Parisian. All the rooms are surprisingly spacious, given the densely built location. Downstairs a cosy fireplace is ideal for a warming winter drink, while in the summer months tables are set out by the courtyard fountain. The rooms lack

the modern sophistications today's travellers are used to, but there is something a little more decadent and – dare I say it – Parisian about having room service bring you up your nightcap. So much love and care has been put into running this hotel, it's hard to believe it only carries three stars.

Style 8, Atmosphere 8, Location 8

Hôtel Grandes Écoles, 75 rue Cardinal Lemoine, Latin Quarter

Tel: 01 43 26 79 23 www.hotel-grandes-ecoles.com
Rates: €115–145

Pass through a large green gateway, and follow an unassuming cobbled path, and you'll reach a small garden, flanked by three buildings belonging to this country-style hotel. You'd be forgiven for thinking you'd just joined the cast of some French family sitcom: the grandmother, son, son's daughter and her children all welcome you in and treat you like one of the family. Although the corridors are in need of renovation (and, apparently, soon will be reno-vated), the bedrooms are delightful – the sort of rooms *The World of Interiors* fantasizes about. The bedrooms, each one unique, all have antique beds and pretty patterned wallpaper, but don't have TVs because the guests

are expected to delight in the peace and quiet of the courtyard – one this size is a rarity in Paris, and you can enjoy breakfast here during the summer months. Take pleasure in the illusion of being secluded, because actually you're not – the lively Place de la Contrescarpe and famed rue Mouffetard are close by.

Style 7, Atmosphere 8, Location 7

Hôtel des Grands Hommes, 17 place du Panthéon, Latin Quarter

Tel: 01 46 34 19 60 www.hoteldesgrandshommes.com
Rates: €215–450

The Hotel des Grands Hommes is situated in a beautiful 18th-century building where André Breton once lived and wrote his Surrealist Manifesto. The 'Grands Hommes' referred to are the luminaries of France entombed in the Panthéon opposite, who include Mirabeau, Marie Curie, Victor Hugo, Voltaire and Rousseau. The Luxembourg Gardens and the tiny streets surrounding the Sorbonne are a short walk from here. The hotel's décor reflects France's glory days, with classic Empire-style decoration. Each of the 31 rooms are slightly different, but all are equipped with standard mod-cons, antique writing-tables and mirrors, bas-reliefs over the beds, and crown mouldings. A neo-classical, spacious lobby and winding staircase add authenticity to a spectacular view of the Panthéon. The sister hotel (Hotel du Panthéon) next door has similar rooms, but they're perhaps a little more floral in style. Both hotels have rooms with a view of the Panthéon, although those without tend to be larger.

Style 8, Atmosphere 8, Location 8

Hôtel du Jeu de Paume, 54 rue Saint-Louis-en-L'Île, Île St-Louis

Tel: 01 43 26 14 18 www.jeudepaumehotel.com
Rates: €255–545. Apartments: €450–900

Staying in a hotel on the picturesque island of Saint Louis is a unique experience, made even more unusual when you discover that the hotel used to be a tennis court in the 1600s. The original *jeu de paume* game was a cross between modern-day tennis and squash – players hit the ball across court

via a wall. The owners have preserved much of the original structure while incorporating modern elements such as a glass lift (from which you can admire the 17th-century timber roof). Enjoying the plain but comfortable bedrooms is not high on the agenda (romantic couples take note); the point is rather to savour the ambience of the whole, which is steeped in character and history. The two apartments, however, are a different kettle of fish altogether: you'll actually feel as if you're living the Parisian dream.

Style 7, Atmosphere 8, Location 9

Hôtel Montalembert, 3 rue de Montalembert, Invalides

Tel: 01 45 49 68 68 www.montalembert.com
Rates: €350–1,250

One of Paris' original boutique hotels, the Montalembert remains high on every chic Parisian's list – and it's in a prime location on the east side of the 7th arrondissement, a stone's throw from the Musée d'Orsay, the shops along the rue du Bac and Le

Bon Marché department store. The entrance hall's pale marble floors make it appear both light and airy, and it's attractively decorated with Oceanic sculptures and exotic plant stems. The hotel suffers from a 'Left Bank Syndrome' of having lifts fit only for the lanky and undernourished, but luckily the rooms are more rounded and expansive. These come in two different styles: the beige-toned, classic, Empire-style room, with antiquated prints in gilded frames, and the minimalist, grey-toned room, with black-framed photography and modern furniture. All 56 rooms are a little different, but room 81 is the one to choose, not only for the view of the Eiffel Tower, but also because it has the largest bathroom in the hotel. The small, charming brasserie is open throughout the day, although they steadfastly refuse to serve dinner during August.

Style 8, Atmosphere 8, Location 8

Hôtel du Petit Moulin, 29–31 rue de Poitou, Marais

Tel: 01 42 74 10 10 www.hoteldupetitmoulin.com
Rates: €180–350

Hôtel du Petit Moulin sits behind the façade of two listed buildings: an old hotel, and what is supposedly the oldest bakery in Paris – dating from the time of Henry IV, it's apparently where Victor Hugo liked to buy his bread. Christian Lacroix has decorated the hotel in a kaleidoscope of different

styles and colours, making each of the 17 rooms unique to correspond with the various facets of the colourful Marais. Brightly coloured Arne Jacobsen chairs contrast with antiquated wallpaper, a classic wardrobe has been covered in graffiti, polka-dot rugs cover parquet floors and vamped-up Victorian

49

bathrooms all point to Lacroix's attempt to nourish the present with elements of the past. The hotel's bar (where you can have breakfast) has been done up to look like a typical trendy Marais café (a pity it's only open to hotel guests), with collages glued onto the walls, a mixed collection of designer chairs, colourful Formica tables and petite zinc-topped bar. Highly recommended – M Lacroix should give up the day job.

Style 9, Atmosphere 9, Location 9

Hôtel des Saint-Pères, 65 rue des Saints-Pères, St Germain
Tel: 01 45 44 50 00 www.esprit-de-france.com
Rates: €125–345

Although Hôtel des Saints-Pères does have its own charm, with its slightly wobbly, original 17th-century staircase and quiet rooms, some featuring wooden beamed ceilings and overlooking a charming courtyard, it is predominantly an ordinary three-star hotel. What makes it unique is room 100 – a pearl amid comfortable but otherwise empty oysters. Referred to as the 'Chambre à la Fresque', it is like a 17th-century ballroom – and the owner's decision not to break the space up by incorporating an open-plan bathroom means you can still waltz around it. It's the creation of Daniel Gittard, archi-

tect to Louis XIV (this was his private residence), and the gold-painted, frescoed high ceilings are glittering reminders of the era's grandeur. The tastefully painted light-blue walls, designer light fittings and Victorian bath, covered in shiny silk drapes and hidden behind a screen for the more demure, make this one of the most original and luxurious rooms in Paris.

Style 8, Atmosphere 8, Location 8

L'Hôtel de Sers, 41 avenue Pierre 1er de Serbie, Champs-Élysées
Tel: 01 53 23 75 75 www.hoteldesers.com
Rates: €450–2,100

Those who remember the former Queen Elizabeth may feel sad to see it transformed by hotel entrepreneur Thibault Vidalenc and architect-brother Thomas into (yet another) designer boutique hotel. The old, cramped and creaking, though utterly charming hotel has been completely gutted to make

way for a minimalist modern look with funky touches. On entering, guests are confronted with an expanse of fuchsia carpet stretched out along a long gallery lined with modern light fittings, grand grey leather armchairs, and white walls decorated with classical portraits (remnants of the old hotel, perhaps?). The fuchsia, grey and white colour scheme is continued throughout the whole hotel, including its bar and restaurant, which look out onto a lovely courtyard, and its no-nonsense minimalist rooms. The suites and one utterly luxurious top-floor apartment have breathtaking views of Paris. There's a small spa, which also offers massages in your room, or the novel idea of 'customized' baths, which are run and prepared for your total relaxation after a hard day's shopping or organizing fashion shoots.

Style 8, Atmosphere 8, Location 8

Kube, 1–5 passage Ruelle, Montmartre
Tel: 01 42 05 20 00 www.kubehotel.com
Rates: €250–750

From the creators of the Murano Urban Resort, Hotel Kube follows a similar concept. The bright rooms, accessed only via fingerprint-recognition ID pads, deliver a sensory overload in contrast with the pitch-black corridors, which are illuminated only by subtle LED disco lights. Once inside, the rooms feature synthetic fur curtains, bedside tables resembling giant ice-cubes, and photographs of hip-hop bling-styled models in bikinis and fur

coats. The hotel's star attraction is the Ice Kube bar sponsored by Grey Goose, where you can enjoy vodka in sub-zero temperatures, wrapped up in a courtesy anorak. The ice references permeate throughout – even the reception is a large glass ice–cube-like square box at the centre of the square-tiled courtyard fronting this ultra designer establishment. The hotel enjoys teasing your senses, from a welcome drink at the ice bar, to the constant flurry of scantily clad models on photo shoots, to the lingering alcohol and smoke odours trapped in the ice. One does ultimately feel as if one is staying in a nightclub or a music video. Although it's close to Montmartre, and walking-distance from the hip canalsides of Bassin de la Villette and Saint-Martin, one might not feel altogether comfortable walking 'home' late at night alone. But, then again, this is as close to MTV as you're likely to get, and that's what taxis were invented for – n'est-ce pas?

Style 8, Atmosphere 8, Location 6

Murano Urban Resort, 13 boulevard de Temple, Marais
Tel: 01 42 71 20 00   www.muranoresort.com
Rates: €350–2,500

Keep your shades on – and not just to blend in with the scene – the focal point of this hotel is a bright, glass-roofed atrium fitted with all-white leather sofas and cup chairs; the only bit of warmth comes from the slick, wall-stretched fireplace. All 52 rooms are luminous, too, with white walls and carpets, which can be differentiated only by the Pop Art prints on the wall. This flash of brightness is designed to contrast with the dimly lit corridors, down which you have to feel your way. This is the hotel's sensuous touch – there's no fumbling for keys here, just a fingerprint ID system that allows you access to your room – which allows for other sorts of fumbling in the dark passages. That's unless you're here on their 'Love&Luxe' package and confined to the honeymoon suite, which boasts its own rooftop terrace with heated pool; here you can savour the complimentary champagne and caviar and stay in bed for the best part of the next day (you get a privileged 4pm checkout). But if you've whiled away the hours in the funky bar instead, rejuvenate yourself in the spa before heading out to do it all over again.

Style 9, Atmosphere 8, Location 8

Park Hyatt Vendôme, 5 rue de la Paix, Louvre
Tel: 01 58 71 12 34 www.paris.vendome.hyatt.com
Rates: €580–1,900

With its creamy French limestone and mahogany interior, and masculine-scented corridors (the perfume was specially concocted for the hotel by Blaise Mautin), staying in the Park Hyatt Vendôme is like staying in a luxury cigar box. This is no bad thing, just an acquired taste, which has been put together by architect Ed Tuttle. The rooms mirror the elegance of the

hotel's communal areas, and, of course, the emphasis is on superior quality (Bang & Olufsen entertainment systems). The hotel boasts its own extensive permanent art collection and has commissioned sculptress Roseline Granet to create signature figurine light fittings and door handles. The courtyard, where one can sip summer aperitifs, is transformed into a winter sculpture garden. Housed within five converted Haussmann buildings, the Vendôme is the residence du choix for elegantly sophisticated business travellers, who are lost without round-the-clock room service and an exclusive spa.

Style 8, Atmosphere 7, Location 8/9

Pavillon de la Reine, 28 place des Vosges, Marais
Tel: 01 40 29 19 19   www.pavillon-de-la-reine.com
Rates: €350–800

The romantic and magical approach to the ivy-covered façade of Pavillon de

la Reine, through the tunnel of colonnades surrounding the beautiful, cobbled Places des Vosges, is soundtracked by the operatic voice of the

local castrato. However, despite such a grand entrance, the interior, elegantly decorated in classic French style, still doesn't disappoint. It's a pleasure to sit in the red-walled bar listening to the crackle of burning wood in the stone fireplace, while sipping a drink poured from the honesty bar (above which an oil painting of a priest is strategically placed, eyeing you up and down, and testing your conscience). The rooms are tasteful and stylish and some even have their own little terraces. The hotel is also ideally placed for those on a mission to explore Paris' nightlife, since it is sandwiched between the lively Marais and the bars of the Bastille.

Style 8, Atmosphere 8, Location 9

Pershing Hall, 49 rue Pierre Charron, Champs-Élysées
Tel: 01 58 36 58 00 www.pershinghall.com
Rates: €420–1,000

This is a hotel geared towards a fashion-conscious clientele who feel at home in Paris' shop-filled 'golden triangle'. Andrée Putman truly shows off her designing capabilities here (many say it is a showcase of her best work), creating an ultra-modern boutique hotel in the shell of what once was the

World War I headquarters of American General Pershing. The courtyard takes centre stage; landscape designer Patrick Blanc has created an ever-green vertical garden made up of 300 different botanical species that climb the stretch of one wall. Sitting next to it, you feel as if the Amazon Basin is starting to take over the concrete jungle. The hotel's bar is a hip party place for the 8th arrondissement, where a DJ spins every night, and the restaurant is very popular for high-design dining. The 26 rooms, kitted out with Bang & Olufsen-style mod-cons, free WiFi and a complimentary mini-bar, are simple, perhaps offering a serene respite from the rest of the hotel, with dark floors that bring out the bright white walls and bed linen. The slate-grey, minimalist bathrooms are kitted out with Talika products from the hotel's spa downtairs.

Style 9, Atmosphere 8, Location 8

Le Placide, 6 rue Saint-Placide, St Germain
Tel: 01 42 84 34 60 www.lepalcidehotel.com
Rates: €350–370

Architect and designer Bruno Borrione, Philippe Starck's right-hand man, is responsible for the mature yet funky look of this small boutique hotel. The lounge is panelled in slick veneer, with matching tables and inviting brown armchairs, and an electric pebble-lined fireplace warms the space up in

winter. The grey walls of the lobby and sober tones of the bedrooms are in complete contrast with the bright colours used for the communal spaces. The smallish bedrooms are plastered in Cole & Sons 'The Woods' wallpaper, while the bathrooms are screened off by a sheet of glass (for the more demure a lush velour curtain can conceal your modesty). Large, elegant white leather headboards, designer wastepaper bins and state-of-the-art plasma TVs enhance the bedrooms. The attention to detail doesn't stop there: the coat-hangers are silk-padded, the key-rings customized, and the breakfast pastries freshly made in the best bakery in Paris. The hotel is ideally suited for shopaholics, since it's literally round the corner from Le Bon Marché; and for the most serious shoppers a VIP check-in/check-out service is available in collaboration with the airport, so you can spend those precious extra minutes finishing your shopping instead of queueing at Departures.

Style 9, Atmosphere 8, Location 8

Plaza Athénée, 25 avenue Montaigne, Champs-Élysées
Tel: 01 53 67 66 65 www.plaza-athenee-paris.com
Rates: €565–10,200

Born in 1911, facelift in 2000. The row of Lamborghinis, Bentleys and Ferraris parked outside (many with Arab state or Swiss number plates) give away the clientele. This comes as no surprise, as the hotel is situated on Paris' glamorous avenue Montaigne, where one can shop at Christian Dior, Chanel, Louis Vuitton, et al. Interior designers Bettina Mortemard and Marie-José Pommereau have completely refurbished the hotel in opulent, modern elegance: gold and bronze finishes, silky curtains, rich fabrics, velvet

furnishings and huge chandeliers (all in the best possible taste). Most of the 188 rooms and suites, which overlook avenue Montaigne, the Eiffel Tower or the hotel's beautiful courtyard, are decorated in rich Louis XVI and Regency style, while two floors are Art Deco. The Royal Suite is the largest suite in Paris: not only does it have its own steam room and jacuzzis, but also a mini-bar for cosmetics and numerous plasma TVs hidden behind mirrors.

The mahogany-panelled fitness centre offers a personal trainer, massage and shiatsu treatments. The hotel restaurant, headed by legendary chef Alain Ducasse, as well as The Bar and the tea salon La Galerie des Goblins, are all worthy of separate mention.

Style 9, Atmosphere 8, Location 8

Raphael, 17 avenue Kléber, Trocadero
Tel: 01 53 64 32 00 www.raphael-hotel.com
Rates: €465–5,450

One could argue that the Raphael was Paris' first boutique hotel (although it has 86 rooms), created by the owners of the then (we're talking 1907) largest hotel in Europe, The Majestic (29 rue Dumont d'Urville, 16th), in response to demands for a smaller, more exclusive place to stay. And what's more, it is still owned by the same Parisian family (Baverez), who built it in

1925. The décor stays true to the original – it's recently undergone a loving restoration that spanned more than a decade. The French walnut-panelled lobby is galleried; the marvellous lifts are still manually closed with sliding barriers; and the stained-glass windows, antique tapestries and furniture are as beautiful as they ever were. The sumptuously decorated bedrooms have high, wooden-arched ceilings, Louis XVI furnishings and spacious built-in wardrobes designed to accommodate the contents of the extensive luggage commonly brought by tourists at the time. The style is actually English, probably because the upper-class Brits from the Roaring '20s were the main visitors then. The Bar Anglais is famous for its cocktails, and the Jardins Plein

Ciel top-floor terrace offers a 360 degree view of Paris; here, you can eat or simply enjoy an aperitif. This hotel is not to be missed: come to visit, even if you're not you're staying overnight.

Style 8, Atmosphere 9, Location 8

Relais Christine, 3 rue Christine, St Germain
Tel: 01 40 51 60 80 www.relais-christine.com
Rates: €355–750

The Relais Christine is a charming hotel on the Left Bank, a stone's throw from the Louvre, the Musée d'Orsay and the Seine. Situated on the quiet street from which it takes its name, it is nevertheless surrounded by lively restaurants and bars (most notably on the famous rue Saint-André-des-Arts). Somewhat incongruously, it started life as a 16th-century mansion built on the ruins of a 13th-century Augustinian cloister, which you still approach through an old courtyard; of the original building all that remains is a copper cooking pot in the breakfast room (which used to be the old kitchens) and a coat of armour. The rooms are decorated in the ever-

popular classic contemporary style (try to book one with gorgeous wooden beams and its own terrace), and there is a wonderful sitting room kitted out with antique furniture and an honesty bar. An incredible spa awaits you in the converted basement vaults.

Style 8, Atmosphere 8, Location 8

Ritz Paris, 15 place Vendôme, Palais Royal
Tel: 01 43 16 30 30   www.ritzparis.com
Rates: €680–2,000

The Ritz stands in the heart of Paris within the elegant place Vendôme. The hotel is famous not only for its position as Paris' leading hotel for generations, but also for its guests: F. Scott Fitzgerald, Ernest Hemingway (giving his name to the famous bar) and, fatefully, Dodi and Diana have all passed through the Ritz' revolving doors. Coco Chanel made it her principal residence from 1934 till her death in 1971, a fact celebrated by the traditional

Fashion Week soirées that take place here. Gastronomic delights are served up at the Espadon restaurant, while a famous people-spotting brunch is taken to the tune of a piano in the César Ritzy Salon. The Ritz' very own Escoffier cooking school teaches professional chefs and amateur enthusiasts alike how to cook like the master; and for the more light-hearted – and lonely – one Friday a month is given over to the 'Ritzy Rendez-vous' (cooking lessons for singles… saucy!). The spa's beauty salon offers nothing less than La Prairie products for both men and women. A palm-tree staircase descends to the fabulous Grecian pool, surrounded by columns and coupled with a convenient bar. Sip cocktails in your facemask wearing nothing but your Ritz bathrobe, and feel like you're a member of the Carrington/Colby dynasty.

Style 7, Atmosphere 9, Location 9

Saint-Grégoire, 43 rue de l'Abbé Grégoire, St Germain

Tel: 01 45 48 23 23 www.hotelsaintgregoire.com
Rates: €185–260

A rather eccentric little hotel run by the equally eccentric Monsieur de Bené
(or 'François', as he might ask you to call him). You'll feel as if you're staying in
someone's 18th-century home. The comfortable sofa-filled lounge is complete
with fireplace, old oil paintings, a jumble of umbrellas and walking sticks and a
variety of objects accumulated over time and arranged in a way that you'd
only find in a private house. All 20 rooms are a little different, although they
share their pink colour scheme and array of antique furniture. Ask for a room
with its own private terrace (specifically, rooms 14 and 16; they're also larger
with magnificently high ceilings). The original creaking staircase remains, which
you descend into the converted old wine cellar, now a breakfast room, where

wicker baskets and straw hats decorate the stone walls. It's also walking-
distance from the glorious Bon Marché department store and buzzing boutiques of the fashionable 6th. A true find.

Style 8, Atmosphere 9, Location 8

Saint James Paris, 43 avenue Bugeaud, Trocadero

Tel: 01 44 05 81 81 www.saint-james-paris.com
Rates: €350–800

A Parisian family bought this 100-year-old château and converted it into a luxury hotel in 1990 – previously it belonged to an Englishman who ran it as an

old-fashioned gentleman's club. The club atmosphere still prevails, with a grand staircase and dark wood-panelled bar surrounded by old bookcases (where you can listen to live jazz every Friday night). A British pillar-box greets you at the entrance gate and an abandoned red phone box stands silently in the garden. It's still run as a private club, and the Parisian elite hold business lunches here (the restaurant is only open to members and

hotel guests). Many of the guests are regulars, always staying in the same room, which gives it an added 'members only' feel, and the sense of exclusivity is compounded by the fact that it is surrounded by high walls and its own garden (it is the only château-hotel in Paris). The rooms are like huge apartments, and those facing the indoor 'winter garden' have their own indoor terraces with armchairs, cornered off by curtains. A small gym and a free sun bed help to gloss over too many late nights.

Style 7, Atmosphere 8, Location 6/7

Saint Thomas d'Aquin, 3 rue du Pré-aux-Clercs, St Germain

Tel: 01 42 61 01 22 www.hotel-st-thomas-daquin.com
Rates: €130

Hotel Saint Thomas D'Aquin is on the beautiful boutique-lined rue du Pré aux Clercs, in an area dominated by antique shops and galleries in the 7th arrondissement, and not far from the boulevard Saint-Germain and Musée d'Orsay. It's a real find, not only because of its location but also because it's both stylish and incredibly good value for money. The lobby and lounge have tasteful, light grey walls, English armchairs and dark wood coffee tables strewn with newspapers and magazines. The rooms, each one unique, are simple, with elegantly  chequered or striped curtains and headboards, French windows with wooden shutters and ivy-topped flower boxes (but perhaps not good for the cruel summer since there's no air-conditioning). Aperitifs can be taken at the bar, they serve a delicious continental breakfast, and what's more, the WiFi's free.

Style 8, Atmosphere 8, Location 8

Sezz, 6, avenue Frémiet, Trocadero
Tel: 01 56 75 26 26 www.hotelsezz.com
Rates: €270–700

Shahé Kalaidjian's second boutique hotel in Paris after Pavillon de Paris is certainly one of the most stunning in terms of designed modernism. The check-in process involves coffee or cocktails, and takes place at the Grande Dame Bar (named after a Veuve Clicquot champagne) – they've scrapped

the idea of a reception desk (too formal). Assistants can be contacted through their walkie-talkies and answer your every beck and call. Each of the 27 rooms is unique, although they adhere to designer Christophe Pillet's formula: low designer beds wrapped in charcoal cashmere covers, surrounded by beautiful imported grey slate walls (in which you can even see the occasional fossil) and tear-drop lamps. Stylish flat-screen TVs and DVDs entertain the bored and the beautiful, while coffee-table books divert the more literary-minded. Thick, fluffy rugs and red or green armchairs and sofas dilute the somewhat masculine look. The opulent bathrooms, with tubs big enough for two, are shielded off from the bedrooms by sheets of glass. The residential location may be a little unusual for a hotel (although the Eiffel Tower is only a short walk away) but the setting couldn't be more intimate and romantic.

Style 9, Atmosphere 8, Location 7

Thérèse, 5–7 rue Thérèse, Opéra
Tel: 01 42 96 10 01   www.hoteltherese.com
Rates: €136–266

If you need a minimalist moment away from the opulence of the Opéra and the frou-frou bustle of the rue Saint-Honoré, then this is the place for you – a quiet, understated hotel, done up in a classic contemporary style, à la Armani. The communal areas are warm and inviting: the lounge has a low, comfortable settee with similar armchairs, a cluster of tasteful pictures, refined dark walnut furniture and parquet floors. The 40 rooms and three

junior suites are dominated by beds with high brown headboards and are more sombre in colour, perhaps even a little bland. Thérèse's strength is in its location – in the heart of the Rive Droite, walking-distance from the place Vendôme, Opéra and Louvre. It also feels far from the madding crowd, tucked away in a narrow side street down which traffic rarely flows.

Style 7, Atmosphere 7, Location 8

Trocadero Dokan's, 117 rue Lauriston, Trocadero

Tel: 01 53 65 66 99 www.dokhans-sofitel-paris.com
Rates: €440–900

This 19th-century building oozes sophistication. Nothing has been left untouched by famous interior designer Frédéric Méchiche, from the hand-made silk curtains to painted wallpaper and carpets, giving the classic look a subtle contemporary twist. The lounge features original artworks by Picasso and Matisse, and a cosy fireplace. The lift is made out of a 1930s Louis

Vuitton trunk, giving a whole new meaning to travel. There are 45 rooms and four suites that reach the heights of comfort and discretion, each one unique in form and decoration, but refined and elegant. La Suite Eiffel (named after its view) is perched at the top of the building – overlooking the rooftops of Paris, and encapsulating the spirit of the city. Appropriately for a hotel that's in a class of its own, it has the only Champagne Bar in Paris, and every Thursday from 6.30pm until 8.30pm you can attend a tasting of vintages (both major and more obscure). The bar is a turquoise wood-panelled room, decorated with gold leaf and oil paintings, both of which shimmer at night when the room is illuminated by an uncountable number of candles. It's no wonder that Mr Armani books the Trocadéro Dokan entirely for himself and his entourage each Fashion Week – the hotel is just like a carefully put together haute couture dress.

Style 9, Atmosphere 9, Location 8

Villa d'Estrées, 17 rue Gît-le-Coeur, St Germain
Tel: 01 55 42 71 11   www.villadestrees.com
Rates: €205–640

Jacques Garcia designed this tasteful and tiny hotel (10 rooms), which sits on a picturesque cobblestoned street in between the animated André des Arts, Saint-Michel and the Seine. The rooms are decorated with fashionable 'English' wallpaper (bold colours and prints), silk curtains, striped upholstery and carpets. Gracious low lighting (cellulite concealing) in the black slate bathrooms are offset by elegant white orchids. Breakfast is served in the entrance lobby, an opulent oriental 19th–century amalgam of black and gold corniccing, neo-classical armchairs and deep red velvet soft furnishings. The owners also run the 15th-century Résidence des Arts opposite, which in the

summer of 2006 underwent extensive refurbishment to match Villa d'Estrées in style and quality, adding a further 11 rooms as well as a brasserie and restaurant. The only danger in staying here is you may never want to leave.

Style 9, Atmosphere 9, Location 9

Villa Royale, 2 rue Duperré, Pigalle

Tel: 01 55 31 78 78 www.leshotelsdeparis.com

Rates: €200–450

Sex, sleaze and show-girls are all words synonymous with Paris' Pigalle district. Villa Royale fittingly sounds like the kind of place you'd go to experience all three. With views of Sacré-Coeur and dazzling neon club lights, it's at a safe distance from the seriously seedy streets (well, just) but close enough for you to feel the thrill of decadence and danger. The hotel is a

tongue-in-cheek reflection of the area – done up like a whore's boudoir. Sexy silk pink padded doors, drapes and wallpaper, rococo gilt-framed LCD screens and fireplaces and bathrooms with jacuzzis for two… Each room has been named after a glamorous celeb: Naomi Campbell, Catherine Deneuve, Serge Gainsbourg – all of whom you can imagine getting kinky in the dimly lit corridors. The perfect place for a dirty weekend in Paris.

Style 9, Atmosphere 9, Location 9

Notes & Updates

eat...

With cities such as London and New York rising to the forefront of cutting-edge cuisine, along with the phenomenal El Bulli in Spain, Parisian chefs have been increasingly criticized for their lack of innovation. Diners were tiring of the stuffy traditional restaurant and the regimented 'entrée – plate – dessert' formula. As a result, 'Le Fooding' was born. Coined by food critic Alexandre Cammas, 'Le Fooding' is an amalgamation of 'food' and 'feeling' that has now become a part of every Parisian's vocabulary (www.lefooding.com).

The concept is that dining should delight all the senses through culinary creations that are both intuitive and inventive, and has turned into a revolutionary movement, with its own annual 'fooding' awards and events. It's more about tasting than eating, which has the added advantage of helping chic Parisiennes retain their svelte waistlines.

In a similar vein, influential food journalist Luc Dubanchet quit Gault Millau (the second most revered critic after Michelin) to start his own food guide, magazine and annual festival (www.omnivore.fr), which recognizes trendsetters such as Inaki Aizpitarte (Le Refectoire and La Famille) and Yves Camdeborde (Le Comptoir de Relais). As a result, many of the haute-cuisine chefs such as Alain Ducasse, while still retaining their haute cuisine in haute-prix establishments, are opening less formal restaurants serving tapas-style entrées that Parisians like to term 'finger food'. 'Le Fooding' has also spearheaded the fusion craze: of the 20,000 or so restaurants in Paris, there probably aren't many that don't feature Asian-inspired tuna steak with sesame seeds on their menu. The upshot is often uninspiring, and you long for a traditional steak tartar. There is no better example of this kind of 'style over substance' establishment than the Costes restaurants.

Because food has traditionally been a feast for the eyes as well as for the palate, the aesthetics of the dining area as well as of the plate have always merited attention. Certain historic interiors, untouched for over a hundred years, such as the famous Le Grand Véfour and Le Train Bleu, have become as famous as the food. Brasserie gems such as La Coupole and Bofinger are worth visiting just for their Art Nouveau, mirror-lined spaces, let alone their colossal seafood bars outside.

Then there are the trendy concept restaurants, some of which come and go; here you either feel as if you're dining in a club or art gallery (La Cantine du Faubourg and Le Cristal Room) or you actually are (Tokyo Eat). Paris also caters for international taste buds, from Jewish eateries in the Marais to Chinese in the Olympiades. But nothing beats an independent bistro that's full of character and fascinating locals (Le Taxi Jaune, Au Pied de Fouet).

The French stick to traditional mealtimes, serving lunch between 12 and 2.30pm and dinner between 7.30 and 10.30pm. For many restaurants, booking even at lunchtime is essential, as Parisians leave their offices to indulge in three-course wine-fuelled meals (it's a wonder how they can get back to work). Brasseries still accommodate eating round the clock: the trendy Le Tambour on rue Montmartre serves food until dawn, and there's always the famous 24-hour restaurant Au Pied de Cochon in Les Halles for night-owls.

In terms of culinary shopping, Paris resembles a giant food hall: the open markets are colourful and beaming with life; saliva-inducing épiceries, fromageries and charcuteries beckon from every street corner; and the boulangeries seem to follow you everywhere, tempting you with the iconic baguette and irresistible éclair.

Prices given are for two courses and half a bottle of wine for one.

Top 10 restaurants in Paris:
1. Pavillon Ledoyen
2. Le Meurice
3. Café Noir
4. Le Comptoir de Relais
5. Le Train Bleu
6. Le Chateaubriand
7. Hôtel du Nord
8. Le Sainte Marthe
9. Anahi
10. Tokyo Eat

Top 5 restaurants for food:
1. Apicius
2. Le Comptoir du Relais
3. Kodo
4. Le Meurice
5. Café Noir

Top 5 restaurants for service:
1. Le Meurice
2. La Crémerie Chaude
3. Le Ciel de Paris
4. Café Noir
5. Pavillon Ledoyen

Top 5 restaurants for atmosphere:
1. La Cantine du Faubourg
2. Le Comptoir du Relais
3. Le Chateaubriand
4. Anahi
5. Le Sainthe Marthe

Au 35 rue Jacob, 35 rue Jacob, St-Germain-des-Prés
Tel: 01 42 60 23 24
Open: noon–midnight daily   €60
French – bistro

A great place for lunch if you're exploring the shops of the quaint little streets of the Left Bank, the charming little bistro Au 35 rue Jacob serves simple traditional French dishes made with the highest-quality ingredients. Sit back and enjoy the subdued atmosphere (the patron has a no-music

policy, promoting the lost art of conversation) among publishing professionals discussing manuscripts and contracts. Not many restaurants offer melt-in-your-mouth foie gras of this quality, complemented with a wine from the carefully chosen list. It's a cosy place, filled with little tables and red banquettes, and original Yves Saint Laurent 'Love' prints of postcards (a gift to the proud owner) give the mirrored walls added colour. The mural of more diners and tables is, no doubt, a trompe l'oeil attempt at making this personal space appear larger.

Food 8, Service 8, Atmosphere 7

404, 69 rue des Gravilliers, Marais
Tel: 01 42 74 57 81
Open: noon–2.30pm (4pm Sat–Sun), 8pm–midnight daily   €50
North African

The 404 is named after the Peugeot car, apparently the transport of choice for migrants leaving Algeria and therefore close to the heart of Algerian-born owner, Mourad Mazouz – who, incidentally, also owns Momo in London. Le 404 is one of the few places that adopts the ubiquitous 1001 Nights décor, typical of Berber restaurants, without appearing tacky.

Wooden beams deck the high ceilings, from which hang beautiful antique Moorish lanterns, and the stone walls from the original 16th-century Marais building add to the castle-like feel of the place. The carved wooden furniture, with very low, comfy cushioned seating, is convenient if you're about to pass out in a haze of food and alcohol. For the more romantically inclined, a rather high mezzanine level will conceal all sorts of sins. The 404 is popular with an achingly hip French clientele and style-savvy tourists drawn by the excellent North-African cooking and arabesque beats. After supper, diners often head off to the cool Andy Wahloo bar next door to continue. You'll need to book ahead (especially for the mezzanine).

Food 8, Service 8, Atmosphere 9

Allard, 41 rue Saint-André-des-Arts, St-Germain-des-Prés
Tel: 01 43 26 48 23
Open: noon–2.30pm, 7–10.30pm. Closed Sundays, the last two weeks of July and August.
€90
French – bistro

With red banquettes, stained-glass windows, open kitchen, Toulouse–Lautrec style prints in ornate frames and a inc-topped bar, Allard is the classic French bistro. Located in the heart of St Germain-des-Prés, Allard is a

tourist haunt. If you are to do touristy, and it's hard not to in this area, you might as well do it here. Other restaurants nearby, such as its frog-themed sister restaurant Roger La Grenouille, are tackier and geared up to plumb the tourist trade. Although they may seem a little expensive, Allard's lunch and dinner menus are actually great value. Chef Dider Remay's highly traditional food is faultless and the motley crew of bow-tied waiters charming. Comfortingly, scattered among the Francophiles, sit the elderly regulars at their usual tables, happily chatting away to your waiter as he serves you.

Food 7, Service 8, Atmosphere 7

Anahi, 49 rue Volta, Marais
Tel: 01 48 87 88 24
Open: 8pm–midnight daily €80
Argentinian

An Argentinian restaurant run by sisters Carmina and Pilat, who joyously

kiss the regulars before thrusting margaritas into their hands and steaks on their plates. The bistro-style tables and chairs fill this old charcuterie, where everything has been left untouched since it first opened 20 years ago. Hidden behind the alarmingly derelict exterior is an old Art Deco ceiling, antique mirrors and cracked and crumbling white butcher's shop tiles. An impressive supply of spirit bottles (whiskey and Havana Club) line shelves around the room, while black-and-white portraits of the two sisters hang from the wall. Mario Testino is rumoured to have taken them, unsurprisingly given that Anahi is a firm favourite among the famous and fashionable (don't even try and blag a table during fashion week!). The menu is a haven for carnivores, from ribs and chicken to the house speciality, fabulous steaks specially flown in from Argentina.

Food 8, Service 8, Atmosphere 8

Apicius, 20 rue d'Artois, Champs-Élysées
Tel: 01 43 80 19 66
Open: noon–2.30pm, 7.30–11pm Mon–Fri. Closed August.   €120
Haute Cuisine

There is something terribly film noir about Apicius: the sound of gravel crunching beneath your feet as you approach this enormously grand 19th-century mansion; the manicured gardens at the middle of which stand over-

sized colourful vases; and the canopied terrace where you can take after-noon tea, or enjoy an aperitif before indulging in the sublime dishes of the Michelin-starred menu. To the right of the foyer and the black modern bar is a long corridor, from which branch off various rooms decorated in a time-lessly classic French style. Don't be surprised if you start to feel like a femme fatale or black-suited hit-man waiting to meet a new client at their exclusive residence or grand hotel: after all, the building is owned by film-maker Luc Besson, who has his production offices above. Reservations are essential.

Food 9, Service 8, Atmosphere 8

Barroco, 23 rue Mazarine, St-Germain-des-Prés
Tel: 01 43 26 40 24 www.restaurant-latino.com
Open: 7.30pm–until the last person leaves, daily   €70
Brazilian

Barroco should be tacky, but somehow it manages to carry off a certain elegance. The interior displays a mixture of colonial style and French classicism, enhanced by oversized architectural features, which give the narrow space a dynamic funkiness. Upstairs, a room has been styled as a faux library – aimed at fat-cat cigar-smokers rather than academics. The principally

Brazilian menu, imbued with further South American influences, offers an amazing range of tapas and home-made tortillas to die for, all complemented by a carefully crafted wine list drawn from the region. Later in the week, supremely talented bossa nova bands really charge up the atmosphere. The informal, family-run vibe is primarily maintained by the older mama, who supervises an array of hip, young Brazilian cousins who buzz around, chatting to each other and to the dressed-to-the-nines Brazilian diners in their native tongue.

Food 8, Service 8, Atmosphere 8

Brasserie Lipp, 151 boulevard Saint-Germain, St-Germain

Tel: 01 45 48 53 91

Open: noon–2am daily   €60

French – bistro

It becomes easy to neglect the traditional brasseries in favour of the many budding designer eateries that have spread like a feverish infection over the city, but one should always pay homage to Lipp – the least commercial of the famous historic brasseries that line the boulevard Saint-Germain. Inevitably squeezed in beside fellow tourists, Parisians still flock here for their regular fix of *choucroute* (Emmanuelle Béart

among them) and other Alsatian delicacies, and the famous millefeuille that tastes like heavenly baklava. This place is genuinely Belle Époque, with original Art Nouveau tiles framing the large mirrors that line the walls, allowing diners sitting on the brown leather benches to spy on who's who and what they are eating. This is not pastiche, but the real thing.

Food 7, Service 7, Atmosphere 8

Le Café Marly, Palais du Louvre, Cour Napoléon, 93 rue de Rivoli, Louvre

Tel: 01 49 26 06 60

Open: 8am–2am daily   €60

French

The waiters must surely be models, moonlighting in sharp dark suits, while the stunning waitresses, more confusingly, are not uniformed, highlighting their attempt to counter tradition. (rather like Pei's Pyramid in front of the Louvre, which this café overlooks). The restaurant's perceived coolness is reflected in its hip chill-out music and menu: tomato with mozzarella becomes 'tomate mozza'. The menu uses lots of quotation marks to impress

on us that the food is above the ordinary – which it's not (try the 'extra' tarama or purée 'tradition'). However, it does cater for all tastes (perhaps because it has to be prepared for the thousands of visitors to the Louvre, as well as Parisians), and for all times of day (breakfast through to dinner). The food is overpriced and somewhat hit-and-miss, but one pays for the view of the Louvre and the Da Vinci coders. It's best not to go inside but to stay out on the terrace (glassed in and heated in winter).

Food 6, Service 7, Atmosphere 9

Café Noir, 15 rue Saint-Blaise, Belleville
Tel: 01 40 09 75 80 www.cafenoirparis.com
Open: noon–2.30pm, 7.30–10.30pm daily   €60
French

A touch of class in the otherwise grungy area of the 20th arrondissement, on a quaint cobbled street down from the church of Saint Blaise, the all-black Café Noir is where the in-crowd of serious foodies come to eat. The seasonal menu focuses on revamped traditional French cuisine with eclectic combinations of spices and vegetables – the robust, winterly dishes include aubergine cassoulets, duck breasts with honey and lavender and cardamom mash. The setting couldn't be more authentically Parisian bistro. A chaotic jumble of bric-à-brac (including an old motorbike) surrounds the diners, while cacti and an impressive collection of coffee makers dress the

windowsills. A multitude of hats and helmets hang from the walls alongside 19th-century posters advertising long-gone brands of drink and old sepia photographs. The flirty staff are unpretentious and fun. Café Noir is a great place for lunch before embarking on the massive Père-Lachaise cemetery, or for dinner before hitting hip club La Flèche d'Or just around the corner.

Food 9, Service 9, Atmosphere 9

La Cantine du Faubourg, 105 rue du faubourg Saint-Honoré, Champs-Élysées
Tel: 01 42 56 22 22   www.lacantine.com   €80
Open: 11am–4am daily

La Cantine du Faubourg's large space is cleverly broken up with white curtains and eye-catching projection screens. The crowd, predominantly a

super trendy mix of models, sports stars and media wannabes, pack the banquettes as the constantly changing light flickers around them, no change then from the waiting paparazzi outside. A DJ-booth adjoining the bar spins out languid trip-hop beats, becoming a little less 'lounge' and a little more house as the evening progresses. A special white-tiled room, somewhat reminiscent of a morgue, acts as a funky and original VIP room or room for hire. The modern French menu offers an array of fusion starters contrasting with more traditional entrees – 'le rosbeef avec mash' as well as seasonal specials. If you don't succumb to the menu you can simply hang by the bar surreptitiously people-watching over the rim of your oh-so-strong martini.

Food 8, Service 8, Atmosphere 8

Le Chateaubriand, 129 avenue Parmentier, Oberkampf
Tel: 01 43 57 45 95
Open: noon–2pm, 7.30–11.30pm. Closed Sundays, Mondays and August.
French/Fusion   €45

With its new management and gastro heavyweight chef Inaki Aizpitarte (ex-La Famille), Le Chateaubriand is causing a bit of a stir. At lunch it's so popular a queue of people wait for tables at the bar. Its new über-trendy

status and excellent food means booking for dinner is essential. The 1930s Art Deco interior is refreshingly simple, and the bare cream walls are punctuated only by a few blackboards listing the dishes of the day. The food is contemporary European, ranging from chateaubriand to Vietnamese stir-fry, and creatively combines ingredients such as tuna and chorizo. The short menu changes daily, so everything is going to be fresh and lovingly prepared.

Regulars of old have already made friends with the new, young (and rather sexy) patron Fred Peneau (Café Burq), and are happy to mingle with his designer crowd following of 20- and 30-somethings. The inexpensive wine list guarantees a lively evening atmosphere, made all the more pleasurable by a great selection of tasty tapas.

Food 8, Service 8, Atmosphere 8

Le Cherche Midi, 22 rue du Cherche-Midi, St Germain
Tel: 01 45 48 27 44
Open: noon–3pm, 8–11.45pm daily   €60
Italian

The food is Italian, the décor French. Green banquettes, Art Deco lamps, fans and caramel walls are reflected in the mirror-lined room. A tiny zinc-topped bar holds a tempting array of prosciutto and antipasti, which, like the rest of the menu, is thoroughly unpretentious. The divine buffalo mozzarella is simply served as a ball and the wonderfully uncomplicated fresh pasta dishes are highly recommended. Because of the restaurant's small size it's always full, down to the pavement terrace where dedicated diners huddle under gas heaters and blankets in winter. Unsurprisingly, the interior is a

seriously tight squeeze and there are no gaps between the tables, so expect to get intimate with your dining companions. Le Cherche Midi has a strong American following, but at least half the clientele will be made up of refined French locals. Booking essential.

Food 8, Service 9, Atmosphere 8

Chez Mai, 65 rue Galande, Latin Quarter

Tel: 01 43 54 05 33

Open: Mai lives in the restaurant, so anytime €15

Chinese

Only an adventurous few will enter Mai's restaurant once they've glimpsed the cupboard-sized space that is largely filled with junk. Those brave enough to visit will, at the end of the narrow wood-panelled room, find an abundance of video cassettes, reams of sewing kits, blue tubs of Nivea, piles of

papers, plastic bags and cardboard boxes filled with God-knows-what, and the token broken radio and telephone. There are only three tables to sit at (the fourth being entirely taken up with more papers, plastic bags, etc.), which are, rather

surprisingly, often full. Mai is an old Chinese lady who's about 2 feet tall and mad as a box of frogs – madness being no barrier to serving up delicious noodle soups and fried rice dishes. She will happily chat to her audience of customers in a mixture of English and French (don't expect it to make much sense or be able to hear most of it, because she insists on calling out through the food portal of the kitchen). Behind a little counter is a 2-foot bed where Mai sleeps. Possibly the most surreal meal you'll have in Paris, or indeed, your lifetime.

Food 7, Service 9, Atmosphere 9

Chez Marianne, 2 rue Hospitalières Saint-Gervais, Marais

Tel: 01 42 72 18 86

Open: noon–midnight daily €20

Mediterranean/Eastern European

Chez Marianne is an institution in the trendy Jewish quarter, which is centred round the rue des Rosiers in the Marais and always buzzing with life. Apart from the terrace seating outside, the restaurant comprises two separate rooms across two buildings, one of which looks more like a wine cellar. The menu combines a mix of Jewish, Mediterranean and Eastern European dishes. Following the mezze tradition, you may choose a mixture of *zakouski* (snacks), priced according to the number of dishes you select. The falafel tastes best in pitta sandwiches served from the kiosk on the street, accompanied by oily aubergines and hummus and tahini sauce –

perfect as a kebab replacement. If you don't want to risk spilling it all down your front, you can sit at a table – but there is an extra charge for this. Customers return time and again, so the staff seem to think they can afford to be a bit brash and very slow… but the really great thing about Chez Marianne is you can eat at any time of day.

Food 8, Service 4, Atmosphere 8

Le Ciel de Paris, Tour Maine, 33 avenue du Maine, Montparnasse
Tel: 01 40 64 77 64   www.cieldeparis.com
Open: 8am–11pm daily   €60
French/Fusion

You are in 1970s heaven here – quite literally, in Europe's highest restaurant, on the 56th floor of the Tour Maine, which you reach by lift in an ear-popping 38 seconds. The starry ceiling melts into the night sky, while the mirrored walls reflect the bright lights of the big city. Gleaming chrome and shiny black cup chairs posed on tan-leather padded balconies separate the restaurant from the piano bar, where you half expect 'Ol' Blue Eyes' himself

to appear. Chef Jean-François Oyon delivers excellent international food with French touches (cod with béarnaise sauce and Chinese peppers, fillet of beef with a truffle sauce), making it a popular choice for Parisians looking to impress foreign guests. Breakfast with a view provides the perfect opportunity for you to plan out your sightseeing schedule on the 3D map of Paris below. Set menus at lunch and dinner make the prices a little more friendly. Booking is recommended if you want a window seat for dinner – but if you really want to fit in, remember to bring your shoulder-pads and sequins.

Food 8, Service 8, Atmosphere 8

Le Comptoir du Relais, 9 Carrefour de l'Odéon, Saint-Germain-des-Prés

Tel: 01 44 27 07 97
Open: noon–6pm, 8.30pm Mon–Fri; noon–11pm Sat, Sun and throughout August   €40
French – bistro

This small Art Deco bistro on the Carrefour de l'Odéon may look like an ordinary bistro, but, as any Parisian will tell you, Le Comptoir du Relais is far from ordinary. This is because it is the venture of Yves Camdeborde, formerly of La Régalade fame, who applies his haute cuisine expertise to bistro cooking at bistro prices (go in the evening for the ultimate culinary experience – during the day the menu is more brasserie in style). As it's achieved cult status, you will have to fight for a table, and with a frequently engaged phone, it's best to make a reservation in person – better still, stay at the

next door hotel run by Yves' wife (apparently, the breakfasts are to die for). Don't bother ordering wine by the glass, even if you are on your own – the bottled stuff is delicious and starts from as little as €15. Even if it leaves your brain a little hazy, you won't be forgetting this delicious country fare in a hurry. Although it's in the heart of tourist land, it's not yet part of the tourist trail.

Food 9, Service 7, Atmosphere 8

La Crémerie Chaude, 49 rue Vaneau, Invalides
Tel: 01 45 44 43 48
Open: noon–2pm daily. Closed August.   €20
French – bistro

You really feel as if you've been invited for dinner chez Yvonne Petit at La Crémerie Chaude, which is simply a room housing four tables and a kitchen. There is no menu, you just get what Yvonne decides to cook that day. Bottles of wine are left on the tables for diners to help themselves, and don't be surprised if Yvonne tries to serve you seconds – she'll decide whether or not you need fattening up. It's a joy to watch her cooking in front of you, partly because the kitchen is no longer confidential as in most restaurants, and because her cooking isn't a show. Yvonne must be pushing 80, so you'll feel guilty about not helping her with the dishes afterwards. It's open only at lunchtime, starting around noon, so try and get there as early as possible before the food runs out. You can call to make a reservation, but

do so in the morning before Yvonne goes to buy her fresh ingredients. If you decide to turn up alone, be prepared to be seated next to one of the regulars and chat away about the events of the day.

Food 8, Service 9, Atmosphere 9

Le Cristal Room, 11 place des États-Unis, Trocadéro
Tel: 01 40 22 11 10
Open: 8.30–10.30am, noon–2.30pm, 8–10.30pm Mon–Sat   €100
French

Baccarat, the renowned French crystal company, has opened an appropriately named restaurant – Le Cristal Room, serving breakfast (for groups larger than 10) as well as lunch and dinner – within its sparkling show-space and plush townhouse headquarters. The humorous, OTT décor is by Philippe Starck, with powder-puff baby-pink benches and cushions, exposed brickwork and ornate marble mouldings. The lighting has been taken care of by

the lavish Baccarat chandeliers, which illuminate the rather bizarre and funky mirrors, crystal objets, oversized pieces of furniture (all created in-house) and the rather elegant crowd. Chef Thierry Burlot produces delicious, playful, very rich French cuisine, and continuing the quirky vein the more sauce-heavy dishes are served in what looks like an upturned German helmet from World War II.

Food 8, Service 8, Atmosphere 8

Curieux Spaghetti Bar, 14 rue Saint Merri, Marais
Tel: 01 42 72 75 97 www.curieuxspag.com
Open: noon–2am daily   €45
Italian

Happily camp boys serve generous mountains of pasta to a mixed, hip crowd while humming to a soundtrack of housed-up disco at this super-trendy restaurant and bar close to the Pompidou Centre. A chain-mail curtain divides the back room restaurant from the bar at the front, although

the neo-baroque funky décor runs throughout. The designer wallpaper changes every couple of months, keeping the look of the place fresh. The menu is strictly spaghetti, served at all times of day and surprisingly al dente given such a high-concept venture. If there's more than one of you (or if you're simply famished) go for the 'marmite' – a whole pot-full from which you serve yourself. With its clubby atmosphere, Curieux is the perfect place to stuff yourself on those essential slow-burning carbs before hitting any dance-floor. If you're not hungry, there's still a great vibe at the bar with a fridge-full of flavoured alcohol-filled test tubes to sample.

Food 7, Service 8, Atmosphere 8

La Fontaine de Mars, 129 rue Saint-Dominique, Invalides

Tel: 01 47 05 46 44

Open: noon–11pm daily €70

French – Gascon

La Fontaine de Mars encapsulates the traditional French bistro-aesthetic: the walls, decorated with mirrors and old sepia photographs, are lined with bench seating, the menu is chalked on a blackboard, the floor is tiled and the tables are covered in red-chequered tablecloths. True Gascon cooking is served to complete the picture, the rich food from the south of France is wonderfully prepared and the cassoulet fantastic. It's so perfectly delivered – with its branded napkins, ashtrays, matchboxes and professional waiters –

you might even think you were in some slick, designer eaterie. In the summer tables pour out of the restaurant into the little square surrounding the eponymous fountain, giving life to a wonderfully communal pavement café. La Fontaine de Mars has been discovered by locals and tourists alike and its popularity with both means that it's a good idea to book.

Food 8, Service 8, Atmosphere 8

Les Fous de L'Île, 33 rue des Deux Ponts, Île Saint-Louis

Tel: 01 43 25 76 67

Open: noon–2.30pm, 7–11pm. Closed Sundays, Mondays and Tuesday evenings. €30

French – bistro

If you'd rather not pay the island's inflated tourist prices for a view of the

Seine and some pretty mediocre cooking, Les Fous de L'Île is for you, as well as being the choice of local Parisians. Although it lacks a picturesque

outdoors the interior is deeply atmospheric, with kooky décor and eccentric, if somewhat laid-back, staff. Built-in display cabinets contain a strange array of crockery, among which sit rather surreal oddities such as a toy caravan and broken telephone. Les Fous is one of the oldest commercial businesses on the island, and the structure has evolved over time: a court-yard was covered and paved to create extra room, and the kitchen used to be another shop altogether. The traditional menu of bistro favourites (think steak frites and salads) is fresh and tasty, but make sure you leave room for the chocolate marvel, the *marquise chocolat*, that is their signature dish. If the chef takes a liking to you (i.e., you're pretty or have eaten all his food) he'll offer you some of his potent home-made Clementine rum liqueur – a potion that has been known to spark off some wild parties here, especially on their Thursday live music nights.

Food 7, Service 7, Atmosphere 8

Le Fumoir, 6 rue de l'Amiral Coligny, Louvre
Tel: 01 42 92 00 24 www.lefumoir.com
Open: 11am–2am daily. Closed 2 weeks in August.   €60
French

Le Fumoir is famous for its Sunday brunches, which attract ladies draped in Gucci and elegant intellectuals scribbling musings into notebooks, who tuck into eggs Benedict and divine pancakes. The casually chic crowd crosses a refreshingly broad age range, where children are seen but not heard and well-polished matrons enjoy Fumoir's celebrated cocktails. There is little pretentious about the restaurant: the waitresses are friendly, the chesterfield sofas and wicker chairs inviting and the food – classic French staples such as foie gras and *filet de boeuf* – delicious. The unvarnished wooden floor and

two ceiling fans rotating in rhythm with the cocktail shaker give Le Fumoir a decidedly colonial feel, as if the restaurant were somewhere between Havana and Indochine. One almost expects Catherine Deneuve to stroll in and share brunch with you.

Food 8, Service 8, Atmosphere 8

Georges, place Georges Pompidou, Beaubourg
Tel: 01 44 78 47 99 www.centrepompidou.fr
Open: 11am–2am daily. Closed Tuesdays.   €60
French/Fusion

Watch Paris expand as you slowly rise up the glass-encased escalators of the Pompidou centre and settle your gaze on one of the most spectacular views across the city. The enormous outdoor roof terrace should be taken advantage of in the summer months, and when the weather turns colder you'll have to stare mournfully out from the window-lined interior. The large rectangular space has been broken up with giant pod-like structures created in glossy aluminium and each coated in a different colour. The futuristic feel of these morphed structures gives you the strange sensation of being enclosed within another organism – very Innerspace, very sci-fi Moby Dick.

As it's coming from a Costes-managed venture, it's not surprising that the French/Asian fusion food is somewhat predictable, the waiting staff slow but super-sexy, as a rather bored-looking DJ promotes their latest CD offering.

Food 7, Service 7, Atmosphere 8

Higuma, 32 bis rue Sainte-Anne, Opéra
Tel: 01 47 03 38 59
Open: 11.30am–10pm daily   €15
Japanese

There is always a lunchtime queue to get into this Japanese noodle 'cantine' – the reason being tasty fresh food on the cheap. Don't be put off by the waiting – the restaurant is deceptively large (three rooms in total) and the swift food turnaround means it'll be your turn next. This is simple no-non-

sense dining, and, unlike some of the other Japanese eateries on the same stretch, no effort has been made with the décor (save one or two ceramic Maneki Neko cats). The atmosphere is created by the loud clatter of crockery in chorus with the chatter from slurping diners. Try to sit in the steamy front room where woks sizzle and spin on impressively large flames in the open kitchen. We recommend the set menus, where you get a delicious dumpling starter and a serving of veg with your choice of noodles.

Food 8, Service 7, Atmosphere 8

L'Homme Bleu, 55 rue Jean Pierre Timbaud, Oberkampf
Tel: 01 48 07 05 63
Open: 5pm–2am. Closed Sundays.   €40
North African

A local bohemian crowd frequents this comfortable North African restaurant to feast on Moroccan food and wine. Without the ubiquitous lanterns and copper plate tables, only a fading desert mural and a few nonchalantly

placed tagine plates give it away as Moroccan. But the food is too good for you to notice the frayed edges, and Malika and her friendly staff offer better hospitality than any décor ever could. Tagines come hot and bubbling to your table and are served with small plates of couscous sprinkled with cinnamon. What's more, food is served right up till one in the morning, which is great if you find yourself getting peckish after exploring the indefatigable bars of the area. Since they don't take reservations, queues often snake out into the street, so you may have to get there early after all.

Service 8, Food 8, Atmosphere 8

Hôtel du Nord, 102 quai de Jemmapes, Canal Saint-Martin

Tel: 01 40 40 78 78 www.hoteldunord.org

Open: 9am–1.30am. Food served daily, noon–3pm, 8pm–midnight. €50

Fusion

Although the Hôtel du Nord is no longer a hotel, the sign on the façade has been listed because Eugène Dabit's novel of the same name, turned into legendary movie by Marcel Carné in the 1930s, is set here. The building's recently been taken over by young and funky entrepreneurs – see their

incredibly hip website – and turned into a restaurant serving a fusion of French contemporary, Italian and even Asian cuisines. Split into two sections, the entrance is more brasserie in style, with white tiled walls and black-and-white floors, a classic zinc-topped bar, a copper coffee machine,  bare tables and mismatched bar stools. The main restaurant at the back is dotted with pieces of reclaimed furniture while still managing to remain minimal and uncluttered. The light grey walls complement the wooden floorboards and the posters and stills from the eponymous film. The restaurant is reserved for the evenings, when the heaving and fashionable crowd creates an atmosphere of 'organized mayhem'.

Food 8, Service 8, Atmosphere 9

Kodo, 29 rue du Bourg Tibourg, Marais

Tel: 01 42 74 45 25

Open: 8pm–11.30pm Tues–Fri; noon–2.30pm, 8pm–midnight Sat–Sun €70

French/Italian

If Austin Powers were a Frenchman – and let's face it, he would be a slightly more refined version of our famous Anglophone – he would be dining at the ultra-lounge Kodo. Comfortable 1960s-style red and white leather cup chairs surround tables set with designer cutlery and brilliantly comic, wonky glasses, while the walls have built-in lava lamps to stare at if conversation runs dry. A long red leather banquette stretches seductively along one wall, teardrop chandeliers hover overhead and orange LED lights on the floor

guide you to the blue-lit loos, where the communal, ultra-modern basins are softened by candlelight. The cuisine is a successful fusion of French and Italian that comes neatly presented in the smallest of portions, and the bar serves up a selection of fantastically crafted cocktails. It's well worth coming for dinner after 9.30pm, when the music is turned up and the mixed 20- to 40-something crowd spills in.

Food 9, Service 7, Atmosphere 7

Maison Blanche, 15 avenue Montaigne, Champs-Élysées
Tel: 01 47 23 55 99 www.maison-blanche.fr
Open: noon–1.45pm, 8–10.45pm. Closed Saturday and Sunday lunches.
Haute Cuisine   €130

The lift doors open to reveal the pure white interior of the Maison Blanche, and you feel as if you've risen to the Pourcel brothers' interpretation of heaven, populated by impossibly handsome men and gracefully chic ladies. The painted floors, high ceilings and fabric-draped columns dazzle in this modern extension, which sits on top of Le Théatre des Champs-Élysées. An expanse of glass allows the diners, like gods, to watch over a magnificent Parisian panorama. The Pourcel brothers focus on a gastronomic juxtaposition of contrasting textures, the idea being that all five senses should be stimulated in one dining experience. The contemporary French haute cuisine mixes dichotomous flavours with contradictory textures, such as deep-fried

courgette flower glazed in honey on a bed of saffron infused purée. One's sixth sense might feel that this is a gimmick, but at the Maison Blanche, the concept works. The one problem with a pristine white interior is everything visibly scuffs – so come in the evenings when Paris, all lit up, shines through the huge window, giving the restaurant a blue glow.

Food 8, Service 8, Atmosphere 8

Market, 15 avenue Matignon, Champs-Élysées
Tel: 01 56 43 40 90
Open: 8am–1am Mon–Fri; noon–11.30pm Sat–Sun   €100
Fusion

A chilled Massive Attack soundtrack and soothingly minimal décor give Market the air of an oasis of calm. This tranquillity has all been orchestrated by French interior designer Christian Liaigre of Marc Jacobs' boutique and

Hotel Mercer (NY) fame. The short, but interesting, cocktail list features exotic mixes of rum, lychee juice and cinnamon, with an equally adventurous menu offering quixotic delights such as raw tuna wasabi cream pizza. The prices may seem a little steep for what it is, but Market is a place to see and to be seen – you just pay a little extra to be among the pretty people. The creative force behind the well-executed fusion menu is Jean-Georges Vongerichten, so international devotees of his New York, London, Hong Kong and Shanghai restaurants will feel instantly at home. Among the highly recommended dishes are the 'Black Platter' starter of spring rolls, dumplings, sushi and other Asian nibbles for two, and the ice cream, elegantly served on a slab of ice. Pierre Hermé pastries are supplied for breakfast and there's an outdoor terrace in the summer, protected from passing traffic by a carefully groomed hedge. Go to Market for dinner before an eventful evening, rather than for an eventful evening.

Food 8, Service 7, Atmosphere 7

Le Meurice, Hotel Meurice, 228 rue de Rivoli, Louvre

Tel: 01 44 58 10 10 www.lemeurice.com
Open: 12.30–2pm, 7.30–10pm. Closed Saturday lunch, Sundays and throughout August.   €225 (Prix fixe €100)
Haute Cuisine

The majesty of the dining room is breathtaking: dining here makes one feel like a royal, an ambassador or an oil heiress – old money, not new, darling. Although opulent, neither the place nor the food is frivolous: each dish is ceremoniously presented by a waiter, matched to the particular course by

rank, who delivers a long and rather poetic description of the chef's creation. The presentation of the incredibly complicated French haute cuisine is as well thought-out as the grooming of the waiters, who move silently and attentively around you like courtiers, bringing extravagant dishes involving poached quails' eggs, caviar and fluffy champagne sauces. You won't be able to sneeze without one of them delicately conjuring up a handkerchief, and you certainly won't be allowed to serve yourself any of the accompanying sauces. Most people's budget will be stretched by Le Meurice, but the experience is worth it: if the Good Lord truly does reside in the subtlest of details, then this is as close as you'll get to heaven.

Food 9, Service 9, Atmosphere 9

Mme Shawn, 34 rue Yves Toudic, Canal Saint-Martin
Tel: 01 42 08 05 07
Open: noon–3pm, 7–11pm daily   €40
Thai

Mme Shawn is not a Thai madame of the sauna sort, but an excellent Thai restaurant famous for its use of fresh ingredients. The innovative menu includes a Thai version of frogs' legs, which makes both the dish and the idea far more palatable. Tastefully decorated, mocha-coloured ceilings and

walls are highlighted with plum tones and Thai wood-carvings, long-stalked exotic plants in over-sized pots and countless lampshades hang from the ceiling. Fairy-lights draped over bamboo screens make it more atmospheric in the evenings (a better time to visit). Boho-chic locals make up the regulars, who cram into this intimate restaurant or chatter animatedly on the pavement terrace in summer.

Food 8, Service 7, Atmosphere 8

Mood, 114 avenue des Champs-Élysées, Champs-Élysées
Tel: 01 42 89 98 89   www.fashion.at/cuisine/2006/mood5-2006.htm
Open: 10am–4am daily   €60
Fusion

Opened in April 2006, this high concept restaurant and bar, located in a small courtyard off the Champs-Élysées, is the first Parisian venture styled by ultra-hip interior designer Didier Gomez. The Mood is 'Asiatique': the upstairs restaurant has a fresh décor of green banquettes, silk cushions, wall-sized photo portraits of kimono-clad geishas and tables decorated with

bonsai trees. Chef Jacky Ribault (formerly of Tsé fame) oversees an interesting menu of French and Oriental dishes, as well as a fusion of the two, such as the mouth-watering steamed dim sum with. Downstairs in the deeply sexy red bar, a hip 20- and 30-something crowd recline on low, bed-style seating hidden in intimate booths, where surprisingly good sushi is served as the perfect accompaniment to the inventive selection of cocktails made with fresh fruits, flowers and spices. The vodka-based Bouquet des Sens, literally pot-pouri in a glass, and the sake laced with honey and lychee juice, both come highly recommended.

Food 8, Service 8, Atmosphere 8

La Mosquée de Paris, 29 rue Geoffroy Saint-Hilaire, Latin Quarter

Tel: 01 43 31 38 20   www.la-mosquee.com
Open: 9am–11.30pm (kitchen closes 10.30pm) daily   €35
North African

You really feel like you've taken a day trip to Morocco the moment you set foot in this peaceful Parisian mosque, founded in 1920 with the support of Arab nations, with its adjoining hammam and restaurant. During the summer, guests sit in the lovely tree-shaded courtyard filled with birdsong, and in winter lounge on comfy cushioned benches amid horseshoe arches, pot-bellied lamps and large copper tray tables. Moroccan, Algerian and Tunisian craftsmen were employed in creating the interior, with its polychrome faience tiles, porphyry stone fountains and cedarwood doors. Succulent pieces of lamb or chicken dressed in rich, tasty sauces are served with couscous or as tagines. The sweet-toothed can sip sugary fresh mint tea, poured

at a great height into delicate glasses, while nibbling on perfumed pastries. Once you've satiated yourself on sticky pastries, sweat the extra calories out at the hammam steam room next door. Try the excellent value 'La Formule Orientale' where, for €58, you get entry to the hammam, a short massage and set menu in the restaurant.

Food 8, Service 8, Atmosphere 8

Le Murano, Hotel Murano Urban Resort, 13 boulevard du Temple, Marais

Tel: 01 42 71 20 00   www.muranoresort.com
Open: 12.30–11pm Mon–Sat; noon–5pm Sun   €80
French

This designer restaurant is part of the designer hotel Murano Urban Resort, and attracts a similarly see-and-be-seen crowd. The smart interior's white marble floors, fuchsia-purple velvet armchairs and banquettes are illuminated by modernist stalactite-like structures hanging unnervingly from the ceil-

ing. Towards the rear, an open terrace is filled with designer outsized plants, while another room is covered with padded walls imbedded with subtly glowing LED lights. The high design is off-

set by a stylishly relaxed atmosphere, enhanced by the DJ spinning funky lounge tunes from a box in the main room. The French contemporary cooking, by two of the scene's rising stars, is geared towards the health-conscious palate of Le Murano's stylish crowd. Less rich than traditional French food, the menu focuses on grilled and steamed fish and meat. The Sunday brunch, packed with glamorous young mothers and less attractive children, allows guests unashamedly to try a little bit of everything.

Food 8, Service 8, Atmosphere 8

My Room, 3 rue Valette, Latin Quarter

Tel: 01 43 26 05 32
Open: 8pm–2am. Closed Saturdays and Sundays.   €20
Japanese

My Room is so small and discreet it's easy to walk straight past – unless you catch a glimpse of the little pink neon 'open' sign in the corner of the window, half hidden by ivy. It's nothing like the other eating establishments of the area, which are dominated by English-speaking tourists, so don't be surprised if you are the only non-Japanese there. The format is typical Tokyo: a wooden bar to eat around, a large 1980s karaoke machine, and a long shelf lined with bottles of Chivas Regal and Jack Daniels, each sporting

a sticker with the regular's name on. Run by a Japanese lady with blue hair, who looks after guests in between tending to her two dogs (one of them so loved her portrait adorns the drinks menu), it's like walking into a Tarantino movie. There is no discernible menu and if you speak no Japanese, you'll just have to point at other people's food or make do with the mixture of sushi, sashimi and noodles that they give you – but rest assured, everything is delicious. You won't get a more authentic experience than this outside Japan.

Food 8, Service 8, Atmosphere 9

Pavillon Ledoyen, 1 avenue Dutuit, Les Champs-Élysées
Tel: 01 53 05 10 01 www.ledoyen.com
Open: noon–2.30pm, 8–9pm. Closed weekends, Monday lunch and August.
Haute Cuisine   €200

Ledoyen's neo-classical building is in itself a promise of a unique dining experience. Located next to Le Petit Palais, on the greenest stretch of the Champs-Élysées, the elegant dining room, with its ornate ceilings and myriad windows, is a delight. The atmosphere, enhanced by the foliage outside that shimmers in the evening light, is simply magnificent no matter what the season. Rebuilt in 1848 after a fire, the original restaurant dates from 1791 and

is steeped in history, having been patronized by the likes of Robespierre and Napoleon Bonaparte and Josephine. The classic French cuisine, with its imaginative, contemporary twists, will not disappoint. The *amuses-bouches* alone are worth coming for, such as the signature *terrine de foie gras* sandwiches and skewered foamy marshmallows. The ever-attentive waiting staff wheel the champagne, cheese and digestif carts around the dining room with great aplomb, and at the end of the meal chef Christian Le Squer makes a point of chatting to all his guests, which is quite unusual for Michelin-starred chefs.

Food 9, Service 9, Atmosphere 9

Pershing Hall, 49 rue Pierre Charron, Champs-Élysées
Tel: 01 58 36 58 00   www.pershinghall.com
Open: 7am–2am daily   €70
French/Fusion

Interior designer Imaad Rahmouni, more recently responsible for Sens (see page 109), has created a sensual quasi-Asian décor. Boxy leather chairs sit on a bottle-encrusted floor covered with plum and fuchsia rugs, and banquettes scattered with Oriental cushions surround the room. The walls are simply decorated with a single, mirrored shelf supporting delicate red Murano glass vases, beside which a white string curtain is caressed by pink and blue hues. Diners also have the option of sitting out in the courtyard to admire the 105-ft vertical garden created by landscape designer Patrick Blanc, made up of 300 different botanical plants climbing over the entire of wall. During the day, when the courtyard becomes a suntrap, you really feel you've discovered a little hideaway from the hustle and bustle of the

Champs-Élysées. A slightly uptight, fashion-conscious crowd are here to 'see and be seen' while they feast on wonderful French fusion gastronomy created by a former Nobu chef. The menu ranges from pure Asian (sushi) to pure French (steak tartare), meeting in between with delicious fusion dishes. The attractive décor and decorous crowd succeed in making you feel rather glamorous.

Food 8, Service 8, Atmosphere 8

Le Petit Marché, 9 rue de Béarn, Marais
Tel: 01 42 72 06 67
Open: noon–3pm (4pm Sat–Sun), 7.30pm–midnight daily   €50
French – bistro

This hip Marais bistro is located just around the corner from the place des Vosges, the oldest square in Paris. Having attracted a fair amount of acclaim

from the international press, Le Petit Marché's clientele has an Anglophone element alongside its bright young French regulars. The short menu offers both classic French fare (*entrecôte* with garlic mash) and Asian-inspired dishes (lightly fried tuna in sesame seeds). The reason everyone comes here is the food – it's generally excellent, and particularly good value for money. Although nothing extraordinary, the décor is pleasant enough: paintings hide most of the wall space and the low, wooden-beamed ceiling creates a warm interior for the winter months. Customers settle down on the red benches where they watch their meal being prepared in the kitchen, and in the summer months there's a marvellous terrace available outside (heated for those chillier evenings), which you'll need to book. Service is friendly but painfully slow, so try to sit somewhere really obvious – such as right under the waiter's nose!

Food 8, Service 6, Atmosphere 7

Au Pied de Fouet, 45 rue de Babylone, Invalides
Tel: 01 47 05 12 27
Open: 11am–11pm. Closed Sundays and Saturday evenings in August.   €40
French – bistro

One of the area's oldest, and smallest, surviving restaurants, Au Pied de Fouet dates back to the early 18th century. Four tables barely fit on the

ground floor next to the size 8 zinc-topped bar, and the upstairs section, reserved for smokers, is a tighter squeeze still. Unpretentious traditional French cuisine is served up on simple tables covered in red-and-white check

105

tablecloths, and washed down with good quality wine. On one wall, next to a rather heavy-duty looking sound system (curious for such a tiny space), is a *meuble à serviettes*, a wooden cabinet with numbered compartments holding the neatly rolled napkins of regulars. It's not a mere decoration stunt, and you'll leave wishing you too had a numbered napkin.

Food 7, Service 8, Atmosphere 9

Le Réfectoire, 80 boulevard Richard Lenoir, Bastille
Tel: 01 48 06 74 85 www.lerefectoire.com
Open: noon–2.30pm, 8–11.30pm. Closed 2 weeks in August. €40
Fusion

The concept behind Le Réfectoire is essentially a 'classroom for adults'. Childish touches – like multicoloured alphabet fridge magnets (spelling out the dish of the day) and oversized molecular models hanging from the ceilings, doubling up as lights in the evening, are mixed in with Cole & Sons wallpaper and Danish furniture, allowing the décor to be playful while remaining designer. The 'trendy art school' aesthetic continues as the bathroom's illuminated floor reveals Lego Star Wars figurines staged on builders'

sand. A mural composed of super-trendy illustrations reflects the 'Grafik' designer crowd. If you're bored waiting for a table, or you've just popped in to sample some of their quality wines (cheeseboards and charcuterie is served throughout the day), you can amuse yourself with the Atari game console by the bar. The large windows give the interior a light, airy feel, and in summer tables are set up on the pleasant, tree-lined boulevard outside. Although they like to think of themselves as something like a trendy canteen, the tasty fusion food with Mediterranean leanings, such as grilled sardines and deep-fried tuna wrapped in seaweed, ain't nothing like school dinners.

Food 8, Service 8, Atmosphere 8

Rôtisserie Sainte-Marthe, 4 rue Sainte-Marthe, Belleville
Tel: n/a
Open: daily, noon–2pm, 8–11.30pm. Closed last week in July and first week in August.   €11
French/Fusion

A crowd of chic bourgeois bohemians migrate from nearby Canal Saint-Martin to the über-grungy but über-trendy street of Sainte-Marthe to join the hippie locals chilling out here. This tiny eatery was set up by the associa-

tion La Rôtisserie Sainte-Marthe as a means of preserving and reinforcing the local community (through meeting, discussion, etc.), which is thought to be under threat from urban regeneration and increasing rents (as well as from the usual suspects, the speed and isolation of modern life). All the money raised by this profit-free organization goes to local charities and projects. Another local organization takes control of the open-plan kitchen each night, diversifying the cuisine. Lunch is reserved for members, but dinner is open to everyone. Come here for the hippie canteen atmosphere, but not for the school-dinner food. Watch out for the crusty with the guitar who'll get everybody (well, the other hippies in the room) singing.

Food 5, Service 8, Atmosphere 9

Le Rousseau, 45 rue du Cherche-Midi, St-Germain-des-Prés

Tel: 01 42 22 51 07

Open: 8am–11pm. Closed Sundays and 2 weeks in August.   €50

French – bistro

Le Rousseau is a bistro-restaurant hybrid. You can eat round the clock with the 'côté brasserie' menu (salads, omelettes, sandwiches): breakfast is served from 8am till 11.30, and aperitifs can be enjoyed in the early evening. Otherwise, during the set Parisian mealtimes, a proper menu of traditional French cooking is on offer. The charming, attentive waiters, dressed in high red aprons and ties, help create an informal atmosphere. Diners sit on wine-red upholstered banquettes at tables set with white tablecloths and red

candles. The mustard-gold walls match the large tubular ceiling lamps, and carefully chosen objects – tea cans, flower vases and books – are placed on sturdy oak shelves, which mirror the bar. The couple who own it really make sure that the food is elegantly presented on refined square plates, and is of the highest quality. The elegantly chic Parisian clientele travel across town to dine here – that's how popular it is – although it's also a real hit with locals. Le Rousseau is a favourite with American tourists and, unlike other more snooty establishments, its staff are sympathetic to their English-speaking customers, cheerfully providing English menus or translations when needed.

Food 8, Service 9, Atmosphere 8

Le Sainte Marthe, 32 rue Sainte-Marthe, Belleville

Tel: 01 44 84 36 96

Open: noon–2.30pm, 8–11pm. Closed Monday and Tuesday lunchtimes, and
from 10 July to the end of August. €40

Italian/French

With its red walls and dark wooden tables, Le Sainte Marthe doesn't charm
you with its designer décor – but after all, it doesn't need to – there's
enough going on outside on the place Sainte Marthe to keep your visual
senses busy. But the food is some of the best you'll find in the area, with its
interesting take on traditional Italian–French cuisine (such as the escargot
ravioli) and large salads served with mozzarella and goat's cheese. The superior wine list makes Le Sainte Marthe somewhere locals can simply pop into
for an aperitif. Wonderfully free of pretension – which can hardly be said of
some of the other places in the area – it attracts an eclectic mix of diners

ranging from moneyed bohemians to, erm, bohemians living on credit. The
outside terrace is a dream during Paris' sweltering summer months – but
book a table, as it gets very busy.

Food 8, Service 8, Atmosphere 9

Sens, 23 rue de Ponthieu, Champs-Élysées

Tel: 01 42 25 95 00

Open: noon–2.30pm, 8–11pm. Closed Saturday lunchtimes, Sundays and
throughout August. €90

Fusion

Sens is a new venture from the Pourcel twins, adding to their already impressive list of global restaurants. Designer Imaad Rahmouni has created a contemporary space where ash grey carpets and furniture are set off by hints of red, from silk cushions to the felt of the pool table. Like the classic

furniture, the food is given a modern twist. The fusion food is inspired by the French colonies and spice routes of the Indian Ocean, where classic French cooking is trans-formed with more unusual ingredients, from fennel to kumquats. But, although the restaurant boasts two Michelin stars (they took one away this year!), the

sweet and sour combinations are often quite hit-and-miss. A mezzanine-level cocktail bar and occasional club night, when tables are cleared and a DJ mixes until dawn, expands the Sens repertoire beyond simply dining. As with all the pricey places in the 8th, expect a slick-suited lunchtime crowd, and elegantly hip evening diners who enjoy posing and pouting in the funky atmosphere and striking décor.

Food 6, Service 7, Atmosphere 7

Le Sporting, 3 rue des Récollets, Canal Saint-Martin
Tel: 01 46 07 02 00
Open: noon–3pm, 7.30–1am dail   €50
French

You can't beat the canalside charm of Le Sporting. Young entrepreneurs Antoine and Sébastien have compiled a delicious seasonal menu of contem-porary French cooking. They've also carefully put together an innovative wine list, posted on a propped-up blackboard, from small but fashionable vineyards across France. Handsome and hip regulars, on first-name terms with the staff, come waltzing in for coffee or aperitifs (so don't be too offended when they get better service than you do). The décor manages an informal chic: the simply painted walls, original oak floor boards and black leather banquettes are offset by an orange globe and the retro font on an old Tarzan film poster. During the day the interior is flooded with natural light through large sliding windows that open up onto a picturesque terrace.

Food 8, Service 7, Atmosphere 8

Le Taxi Jaune, 13 rue Chapon, Marais
Tel: 01 42 76 00 40
Open: noon–3pm, 8–10.30pm. Closed Saturdays and Sundays. €40
French

In the middle of the dusty, narrow Rue Chapon, famed as the district of wholesale handbag sellers, sits the Taxi Jaune bar and restaurant. The interior has largely been left untouched since it opened in 1934: mustard walls, temporary art shows, red table-tops, mosaic floor, large front windows and a counter with a neon halo. Its worn-out look imbues it with bags of character. It's now run by dynamic young chef Otis Lebert, who has worked

alongside Michelin-starred chefs in the UK, Belgium, and Italy, and the traditional French cuisine, with its international twist, is faultless. Loved by the trendy locals of the old Marais quarter, as well as the elderly regulars who look like they've been coming since 1934, it's also the unlikely favoured haunt of fashionistas during Paris Fashion Week. In between busy meal times, it's a peaceful place to enjoy an afternoon beer while soaking up the unique atmosphere.

Food 8, Service 8, Atmosphere 8

Tokyo Eat, Palais de Tokyo, 13 avenue de President-Wilson, Trocadéro

Tel: 01 47 20 00 29 www.palaisdetokyo.com

Open: noon–3pm, 7.30–11.30pm Tues–Sat; noon–5.30pm Sun   €60

Pan-Asian

Tokyo Eat is the restaurant situated inside the contemporary art gallery Palais de Tokyo, offering contemporary dining to match its ultra-designer interior. The menu is 'global', however – chicken combined with basmati, plantain or satay sauce, simply grilled or as a curry – although more conser-

vative antipasti and a few sympathetic veggie options do feature. Lamps, reminiscent of giant Smarties, looming down like spaceships from the amazingly high ceilings, have been designed by contemporary artists, along with the tables, chairs and surrounding artworks. The long rows of round tables, constantly filled by a crowd of aesthetes, run alongside the animated, stainless-steel open kitchen. Eat here and you get reduced entry to the Palais de

Tokyo art gallery, or alternatively opt for the 'lunch menu', which includes free entry, the dish of the day and a coffee, all for a meagre €15. During the summer months Tokyo Eat opens a wonderful terrace overlooking the Seine, where you can enjoy snack food from the gallery's canteen throughout the day.

Food 8, Service 8, Atmosphere 8

Le Train Bleu, place Louis Armand, Bastille
Tel: 01 43 43 09 06 www.le-train-bleu.com
Open: 11.30am–3pm (2.30pm Sun), 7–11pm. Closed Sundays and July to September (dates vary each year).   €75
French

It's an indisputable fact that the Belle Époque interior of Le Train Bleu, designed for the 1900 Universal Exhibition, is unparalleled in the whole of Paris, possibly the world. Huge arched windows are hugged by thick red curtains; smiling cherubs and naked ladies decorate the walls in rococo splendour; and banquettes are made to look like train seats, complete with coat and bag racks overhead. Forty-one spectacular Impressionist frescos lit up by electric Art Nouveau lamps retrace the journey made by the trains of the then famous Paris–Lyon–Mediterranean railway (blue train, of course). It's not surprising that this is the only restaurant in France to have been inaugurated by a French president, Emile Loubet, in April 1901. But it seems a shame that certain details – such as the laminated cards advertising Train Bleu memorabilia – prevent this from being the truly magnificent restaurant

it deserves or has the potential to be. Respected chef André Signoret has brought the classic French fare back to its former glory (there was a time when the décor outshone the food) and the tartare is one of the best in Paris. On the down-side, although the wine list is excellent, it is pricey. We recommend coming here for lunch, when the locals outnumber the tourists passing through. Film-lovers might recognize the interior from a scene in Luc Besson's *Nikita*.

Food 8, Service 8, Atmosphere 9

Ziryab, Institut du Monde Arabe, 1 rue des Fossés Saint-Bernard, Latin Quarter
Tel: 01 53 10 10 16 www.yara-prestige.com
Open: noon–2.30pm, 3–6pm and 7–11pm. Closed Sundays and Mondays.
North African   €80

It would be hard to find a more romantic spot for dinner on a summer's evening than on the 9th-floor roof terrace of the Institute du Monde Arabe – where one can enjoy delightful North African cooking while gazing at a grape-fruit-coloured sun spilling its warm light over the land-mark rooftops of Paris. Even on balmy evenings, a

breeze can threaten to whisk a salad leaf or light slip of pitta off to the next table, so come prepared with additional clothing to drape over you. The food, while more expensive than the Mosquée, isn't necessarily better – but guests really come for the view. The décor, inside the restaurant, is a bit hit-and-miss – a dark pink, star-patterned carpet in need of revamping clashes with the rather shiny red and yellow drapery covering the chairs – but the predominantly Parisian crowd bring their home-grown elegance to the place.

Food 7, Service 7, Atmosphere 8/9

Notes & Updates

drink...

Signed-up members of AA should really stay away from Paris, where you can buy a drink anytime of the day or night. First stop is the café, which does not translate into our 'coffee shop' understanding of the word. Walk in early in the morning, and one comes face to face with a traditional zinc-topped bar leant on by locals sipping their first espressos (the standard coffee, unless stated otherwise). The café then caters for the lunch and dinner crowd, but serves as a bar throughout the day, welcoming drinkers to sit, sip and swallow watching the world go by. Different tariffs (levied on the drink) apply depending on where you stand or sit: you will be charged less if you stand at the bar, while sitting on a terrace outside at a table will be your most expensive option.

The styles of café vary as much as the tariffs. While any two cafés can look very much alike, the crowds can be so wildly different as to give the place its own identity, differentiating a locals' public house from a city hotspot such as Café Charbon in Oberkampf or La Perle in the Marais. Cafés usually shut at 2am, with the exception of the 24-hour ones that only shut for half an hour a day to take advantage of some legal loophole.

Bars, unlike cafés, open between 6pm and 6.30pm and usually see their last customer out at anytime between 2 and 4. The snacks served in bars pale in comparison with the plates of charcuterie and other nibbles offered in cafés or in the dedicated wine bars such as Le Rubis on the marché Saint-Honoré, Café La Fusée near the Centre Pompidou or Habibi in the Bastille. The cheapest plonk in these places is likely to be better than most wines served in a bar in England or the US. Most bars play their music loud: some will have DJs every day, others only at weekends. Some feature live bands and others feel more like a club.

The 'high-end' glitzy bars seldom stand on their own: they are usually affiliated to a restaurant or hotel. If you're a lounge lizard, then head for swanky bars like the one below restaurant Moods; if you're after the cocktail to end all others,

then go to the Hemingway Bar at the Ritz or the bar in the Plaza Athenée.

Drinking begins with aperitifs around 6pm, when many bars offer a 'happy hour' or two of discounts. Those out on a bar crawl should consider the rue Montmartre or the Marais, as they are full of watering-holes, but you can't beat the Oberkampf area for a serious bender. Streets to focus on are Oberkampf, Jean-Pierre Timbaud and Saint-Maur. The highest concentration of bars is on rue de Lappe in the Bastille, but they are mainly of the Havana-themed type, rather tacky and only worthwhile if it's a Bacardi Breezer you're looking for.

L'Alimentation Générale, 64 rue Jean-Pierre Timbaud, Oberkampf

Tel: 01 43 55 42 50

Open: 6pm–2am. Closed Sundays.

Hidden behind the original shop front of this former general store is an incredibly vibrant bar. The space is large, smoky, extremely dark and busy with the Oberkampf-Ménilmontant in-crowd. Sit around the long, wooden

table and sample some of the own-brand beer made with exotic and unusual ingredients such as apricots and basil. The music is a mixed bag (from Blondie to techno), but whatever it is, it's played loud from the DJ booth. The live gigs are also extremely popular, often resulting in a one-out, one-in policy.

Andy Wahloo, 69 rue des Gravilliers, Marais

Tel: 01 42 71 20 38

Open: 6pm–2am. Closed Sundays.

Furnished with old barrel stools and hard benches, Andy Wahloo isn't the most comfortable bar in Paris, but it does serve the best mojitos in town. The style is funky arabesque, with lime-green walls and an innovative use of lanterns and old shop signs for tables. Posters advertising Turkish cigarettes or tinned tomatoes adorn its walls; asymmetric shelving with colourful packaging and products covers the windows. Even the lavatory sign is in Arabic. You can enjoy Moroccan mezzes, supplied by the '404' restaurant next door, since it has the same owner (who also owns Momo and Sketch in London).

It's great to sit outside in the little courtyard during the warmer months, although booking a table in advance is recommended. The music's good, and can be anything from Curtis Mayfield to harder hip-hop beats. It attracts a young crowd, who are rather overshadowed by the trendier staff.

L'Armagnac Café Bar, 104 rue de Charonne, Oberkampf
Tel: 01 43 71 49 43
Open: 7.30am–2am Mon–Fri; 10.30am–2am Sat–Sun

Why is L'Armagnac regularly packed while the more picturesque bistro around the corner, Chardenoux (1 rue Jules Valles, tel: 01 43 71 49 52), once used as a film set by Hitchcock, remains half empty? Perhaps with its low-volume dance music and dim lighting, it is simply less uptight and more inviting to a young drinking crowd attracted by the reasonably priced wines and beer. If you opt to eat at all, go for the handsome planches of cheese and

charcuterie, magnificent croques and huge salads. The space, crammed with tables, is delineated by large Art Nouveau French windows, which can open up wide during the summer months. The eclectic décor adds to the relaxed atmosphere – snooker cues decorate one wall (although there's sadly no table to play on), and there's a small, curved banquette that has a magazine mural that's so old and faded it's hard to tell what it actually is.

L'Assignat, 7 rue Guénégaud, St-Germain
Tel: 01 43 54 87 68
Open: 9.30am until the last person leaves

This microscopic, family-run bistro and wine bar is a well-kept secret among local gallery owners and art students from the nearby Beaux-Arts, who will come here for a simple lunch of 'steak et frites', cooked to perfection and downed with a glass of Bordeaux. The yellowing, nicotine-stained walls, covered with images of coins and bank notes (the Musée Hôtel des Monnaies is

just opposite), red-benched booths and marble-topped tables give the place a true Parisian character. It's a great place to come for reasonably priced coffee and a game of table football, or to perch at the bar with a beer, ridding your pockets of spare change through the jukebox. For the record, if the family granny's there, sitting at one of the booth-banquettes peeling spuds, she doesn't have Tourette's syndrome – it's just that she likes to sporadically give her opinion on whatever conversation you're having at the bar. And don't be surprised if ayou find a dog lying where you want to sit.

Le Bar du Marché, 75 rue de Seine 75006 (on the corner with Buci), St-Germain

Tel: 01 43 26 55 15

Open: 8am–2am daily

Don't be dissuaded by the waiters' questionable uniform of dungarees and

cap, this bar is the
most popular kid on
the block. The interi-
or pays homage to an
American road diner
– think white-striped
leather banquettes
and a neon pink light
above the zinc-topped
bar. Otherwise, it's a
typical mirror-
wrapped French café,

with mosaic floors, vintage posters and Deco light fittings (although a disco
ball that hints to a younger clientele). It's always busy with bright young
things, who mainly flock to the enormous terrace but who will also fill the
interior at night and in winter. It's best to stick to beer or wine since the
cocktails are not up to scratch, but the atmosphere is second to none and
it's certainly THE place to stop off for drinks if you're roaming the cobbled
streets of Saint André des Arts.

Ba'ta'clan Café, 50 boulevard Voltaire, Oberkampf

Tel: 01 49 23 96 33

Open: 8am–2am daily (8am–11.30pm throughout August)

This lovely café/bar screams comfort, with its large, battered, brown leather
sofas and heated terrace, where locals come to chat for hours over one
coffee (perhaps because by local standards it's a rather expensive coffee). Its
style is a deliberate mish-mash with an incongruous but interesting mix of
pagoda and classical Greco-style columns (that apparently used to belong to
an old theatre), yellow walls with substandard art works and an absolutely
immense central bar manned by friendly and trendy staff. As a design ethos,
it doesn't really work, but for whatever reason it summons a smile rather

than a 'tut-tut'. Head here for a daytime coffee or to munch on a late-night croque against the backdrop of an eclectic soundtrack, which mirrors the club nights that take place in the concert-club venue of the same name.

Le Brébant, 32 boulevard Poissonnière, Grands Boulevards
Tel: 01 47 70 01 02
Open: 7.30am–6am daily (happy hour: 7–9pm)

Le Brébant is home to one of the longest bars in Paris – a wave-shaped, zinc-topped bar, behind which are large, arched, gilt-framed mirrors that leave you feeling that you have stumbled on a contemporary reinterpretation of Manet's *Le Bar aux Folies-Bergères*. External ventilation pipes and a

hooped steel railing lend this place an industrial Gaudi-esque feel, while the décor is finished off with multicoloured Habitat steel chairs, classic wooden tables, and a very, very long red bench. In summer, Le Brébant extends out onto the wide pavement, turning it into a high-capacity terrace. A plethora of different sized bulbs suspended at different lengths enliven the ceilings, from which hang two large and rather unnecessary flat-screen TVs (it's a bit tacky – but this is an increasing trend in Parisian bars). With a music policy of lively dance music and an ideal location opposite clubs Pulp and Vinyl (Triptyque is also around the corner), it's the perfect place for pre-clubbing drinks. Amazingly long opening hours (it only shuts for an hour and a half, between 6am and 7.30pm) also make it a popular destination for a post-clubbing breakfast.

Café Charbon, 109 rue Oberkampf, Oberkampf
Tel: 01 43 57 55 13
Open: 9am–2am (4am Thurs–Sat)

Café Charbon can be credited with kickstarting Oberkampf's cool image, and although it has inspired many similarly styled establishments to open in the area, it remains the leader of the pack. Set in a wonderful Belle Époque interior, it comes complete with murals of Moulin Rouge-style dancers, Art Nouveau trimmings and industrial lamps and clocks of the period. Local

trendies take over the bench booths or sit on the terrace to watch the world go by. It's a wonderful place to come for a leisurely breakfast or to pose at the bar for hours smoking rollies with everybody else. The cocktails are potent, the wine selection excellent (although a little pricey) and the food's not bad. Annexed to the cool club Nouveau Casino, it is packed at night with a pre-clubbing crowd.

Café Chic, 126 rue du Faubourg-Saint-Honoré, Champs-Élysées
Tel: 01 45 63 69 69
Open: 8am–5am Mon–Sat; noon–6pm Sun

This is a handy joint to know, since it serves food right up until four in the morning. What's more, you can wash it down with some amazing cocktails or one of the many alcohol-free, fresh smoothies on offer if you're feeling

the worse for wear. DJs play and party here almost every night of the week, and it's obvious from the scratches on the black lacquered tables and the knowing, slightly haggard-but-chic look in the eyes of the waiting staff, that the establishment has witnessed some impromptu decadence. Gold lamp bases designed in the shape of machine guns complement the fuchsia ceilings and black-painted walls, and there's an upstairs room to accommodate the crowds when the party really kicks off.

Café La Fusée, 168 rue Saint-Martin, Beaubourg/Marais
Tel: 01 42 76 93 99
Open: 5pm–2am daily

A wonderful haven in the otherwise touristy, hit-and-miss, bar-filled Beaubourg area around the Pompidou Centre. Café La Fusée is refreshingly simple and laid back, with shelves of broken-spined, battered novels, warm orange-toned walls, and blackboards that offer a vast choice of quality wines along with bar snacks of sandwiches, and cheese or ham platters. The bar area forms an intimate space of high-raised tables, stools and benches, at the back of which is a display cabinet full of inviting wine bottles and posters of past and present exhibitions at the Pompidou Centre. A cool, young, hard-drinking crowd flocks to the long, oak bar-top and fill the terrace outside. It's got a good

atmosphere, and the fact that the wall clock is broken suggests that people come here not to kill a few hours, but to lose themselves in the moment.

La Caravane, 35 rue de la Fontaine au Roi, Oberkampf
Tel: 01 49 23 01 86
Open: 11am–2am Mon–Fri; 6pm–2am Sat–Sun. Closed two weeks in August.

This bar-café-restaurant, just off avenue Parmentier in the trendy 11th arrondissement, is a joyous mix of arabesque crossed with Caribbean cool. The décor is a complete mish-mash, with walls painted in different happy colours, funky wall-papered shelves, and furniture ranging from battered Formica to wicker armchairs. A yellow concrete bar is manned by the friendly dreadlocked Alexis, who makes fabulous fresh fruity cocktails against a soundtrack of ultra-lounge beats. Life is so relaxed here; friends, who

include local DJ Moulinex, just turn up unannounced with a bag of tunes. Don't get confused if 'a pint of cabbage' or 'pigs' brains' comes up on your bill, as they've replaced the beer name-tags with old labels from a general food store. You can't help leaving this joint with a big smile on your face.

Chai 33, 33 Cour St Émilion, Bercy Village, Bercy

Tel: 01 53 44 01 01   www.chai33.com
Open: noon–2am daily (Sunday brunch: noon–3pm)

Chai 33 is all about wine; even the cocktails are wine-based. After a little guided tour of the downstairs cellar, where wine is sorted by colour, taste and global region, your choice is brought up to you in a carafe. However, if you're too lazy to venture down there, colour-coded menus are supplied. There are three wine-tasting sessions a night, at 7pm, 7.30pm and 8pm. In the roomy bar upstairs the vibe is very laid back, while the restaurant on the ground floor is brightly lit and filled with lively, wine-fuelled gossip. Twice a month they stage a crazy take on karaoke, when you can have a go at singing chansons français with a three-piece band. Don't expect to be hand-

ed the mic as you come waltzing in – you need to send in a demo tape beforehand. Screening the good amateur singers from the bad results in quality music, so look out for the dates when the season's finalists fight it out for the title. Make sure you check out the conceptual loos (especially the men's) before you leave.

Chez Prune, 71 quai de Valmy, Canal St-Martin
Tel: 01 42 41 30 47
Open: 8am–2am Mon–Sat; 10am–2am Sun

It's hard to resist the laid-back charm of Chez Prune, which explains why the bar is a favourite for most of the bright young things in Paris. Once you've been here you'll find yourself coming back again and again. Bistro

benches, mosaic floor, a zinc-topped bar, yellow walls decorated with retro clocks and blackboards all give it character. The wine here is excellent, the beer is cold. What more could you want? Bar snacks? Well, Chez Prune triumphs with something better than just your average serving of peanuts: you can nibble on great charcuterie, or sample their 'trois couleurs' (houmous, olive tapenade, taramasalata with bread) or crudités with cream-cheese dip sauce. You can eat lunch here too, and although the food isn't amazing, the canalside terrace is a popular destination.

Dédé la Frite, 52 rue Notre-Dame-des-Victoires, Grands Boulevards/Bourse
Tel: 01 40 41 99 90
Open: 8am–1.30pm daily

This is the kind of bar that you pop into for one drink and end up staying till closing-time. By the third bottle of wine, the little corrugated-iron cubical producing the best French fries in Paris is irresistible – or perhaps you'll find yourself tucking into proper grub in the form of grillades and salads (served until 11pm). During the day this dual aspect bar is filled with natural light, but at night it's comfortably dark. Red and yellow lightbulbs dimly reveal the bare concrete ceiling with exposed ventilation pipes, distressed furnishings and flaking paint, all which give off an 'Ost Berliner' feel. A cool, casual

crowd, wearing battered leather jackets and hoodies, occupies the long dark bar to one side or takes up the mish-mash of tables. Owned by the same team that's behind the lively Pigalle bar La Fourmi (see page 131), it has that same, laid-back vibe. Cheap drinks and decent music make this a winner.

De la Ville Café, 34 boulevard Bonne-Nouvelle, Grands Boulevards
Tel: 01 48 24 48 09
Open: 11am–2am daily

De la Ville Café suffers from a multiple personality disorder. A stunning Belle

Époque bar, with intricate cornicing, dazzling mosaics and a terrace, is divided from a relatively tame, warm and wood-panelled restaurant by a grand staircase that leads up to a lounge and exhibition gallery. Then there is a clubbier room at the back that looks like a children's play area from the 1970s. It's a stylistic mish-mash; red cushions and benches circumnavigate the Danish-style wood panelling, and light-boxed photographs on the walls sit alongside an array of taxidermy. But no matter which space you choose to get comfy in, the crowd's going to be cool and the DJs (Thurs–Sat) are bound to get them dancing.

Les Étages, Saint-Germain, 5 rue de Baci, St-Germain
Tel: 01 46 34 26 26
Open: 11am–2am daily

Along with the nearby Bar du Marché, Les Étages is another popular choice with the 6th arrondissement in-crowd, who fill the small, circular, multi-coloured seats that resemble makeshift drum-kits or oversized bottle tops on the terrace. The seating inside is more comfy, with white, low-sunk armchairs and low, round, red tables. The interior is small, intimate and full of character with bare, creaky floorboards and red walls. There's an extensive cocktail list, but you don't have to queue at the bar since there is table serv-

ice. The sister bar (35 rue Vieille-du-Temple, tel: 01 42 78 72 00; open daily, 3.30pm–2am) in the Marais follows the same formula, although on a larger scale.

Favela Chic, 18 rue du Faubourg du Temple, Oberkampf
Tel: 01 40 21 38 14 www.favelachic.com
Open: 7.30pm–2am daily (4am at weekends). Free entry Tues–Thurs.

The only thing 'favela' about Favela Chic is that it's cramped and crowded (and so perfect for pickpockets); it's also impossible to tell where the 'chic' comes from – apart from the clientele. Substandard – although admittedly potent – cocktails are retrievable from the bar, which is lit by a selection of rather funky upside-down lamps and a disco ball; otherwise the décor is a half-hearted attempt at religious kitsch. Necking couples lean on the speakers, while those that have had a few too many will boogie to a rather

predictable choice of Latin tunes mixed with an ironic mixture of old-school classics. But it must be doing something right or the flock of pretty people wouldn't have been coming here over the years, nor would it have had the means to relocate to a bigger space and open a sister club in London's trendy Shoredich. Expect queues as well as an entrance fee on Friday and Saturday nights. The popular restaurant is a glorified Nando's, with large benches and unforgiving lights.

La Fontaine, 20 rue de la Grande aux Belles, Canal St-Martin
Tel: 01 42 45 36 27 www.laboratoiredelacreation.org
Open: 7.30am–2am daily

Tucked away beyond the cool, canalside cafés of Saint Martin, up an unremarkable street past the Hôpital Saint-Louis, this small bar is more reminiscent of an Edwardian pub than a Parisian joint. The tiny but airy room has large windows on two sides and a brass-topped bar. For the past four years it has been run by two brothers of North African origin who have a

penchant for young and experimental jazz. An intellectual-boho audience come for the performances, which kick off most nights from 9.30pm (except Sundays and throughout August); the musicians vary on a regularly, if not nightly, and entrance is free, although the younger brother walks around, hat in hand, at the end of the evening to collect 'tips' from appreciative patrons. It's also a good option for breakfast and lunch, with speciality couscous served up on Thursdays and Fridays. There are three different beers on tap and a short but comprehensive cocktail list. A place for jazz virgins and aficionados alike.

La Fourmi, 74 rue des Martyrs, Montmartre
Tel: 01 42 64 70 35
Open: 8am–2am Mon–Thurs; 8am–4am Fri–Sat; 10am–2am Sun. Closed 24–25 December.

It is definitely worth a trip to this lively Pigalle bar that's permanently filled with a cool casual crowd sipping coffee or eating lunch, or getting down to the business of some hardcore night-time drinking. It's light and airy during the day, thanks to its large windows, and packed at night. Bowie-rock beats off its dirty yellow walls and huge industrial lamps, mismatched chairs and tables complete the battered look. Temporary artwork by local artists is randomly hung about the place (they don't take a commission, and you get the feeling they're trying to help out a mate), an immense sculpture of wine

bottles hangs from the ceiling, and there is a mezzanine non-smoking level at the back from which you can observe the hustle and bustle. You wouldn't think it, but real effort is put into the cocktails, in case you don't fancy a wine or beer.

Habibi, 44 rue Traversière, Bastille
Tel: 01 53 17 64 12
Open: noon–2am daily; 6pm–2am throughout August

The prime seat in this tiny Bastille wine bar is the makeshift sofa along the huge window; the seats are made of carrier bags and cushions consist of all kinds of fabrics. Otherwise, there are a couple of tables and bar stools to perch on, all made by French artist-designer Dominique Petot using recycled materials. There is a refreshingly short but comprehensive wine list that doesn't break the bank, and the staff are only too happy to advise. It's worth

calling up to find out if you can catch one of their live music evenings, (usually this constitutes a one-man band, since the space is so small), which lend the place added atmosphere and a buzzing crowd. Mezze and a daily speciality Niçoise dish (the

patron is from Nice) are available at lunchtime if you're in need of some of
good, home-cooked grub. The bar is frequented by locals and mates of the
barman, and is often packed out. If it's full and you're in the mood for a glass
of wine, a good second choice is the nearby Le Baron Rouge (1 rue Th.
Roussel, tel: 01 43 43 14 32).

Ice Kube, 1–5 Passage Ruelle, Montmartre

Tel: 01 42 05 2000   www.kubehotel.com
Open: 6.30pm–1.30am daily

On a dark street in the 18th arrondissement, concealed behind gates and
Matrix-style bouncers, is the Kube hotel's dark 15m-long bar, accessorized
with synthetic fur sofas, cubic chairs and blacked-out walls studded with
plasmas, and thronged out with a trendy crowd. To reach the Ice Kube bar,
made (unsurprisingly) entirely of ice, head up the stairs to the walkway balcony. You then pass through the cloakroom to wrap up warmly in an anorak,

hat and gloves before joining the hazy shadows on the other side of the ice
wall. The temperature inside the sealed bar prevents you from drinking the
sponsor's vodka (French company Greygoose) for longer than half a hour,
which is the time slot allocated for each visit, as the space can only hold up
to 20 people. It's decorated with ice sculptures crafted by hip contemporary
artist, Laurent Saksik, and even the cube-shaped shot glasses are made of
ice. Finger food consists of artfully presented frozen sushi, and there's a creative variety of vodka flavours to wash it down. Reservations are obligatory,
and admission to the Ice Kube bar is €38 per person for half an hour.

Le Kitch, 10 rue Oberkampf, Oberkampf
Tel: 01 40 21 94 41
Open: 6.30pm–2am daily

This little bar-cum-restaurant is situated on the calmer side of the rue Oberkampf, by the boulevard Voltaire. Although it's called Le Kitch, the décor isn't OTT: it's rather cool, with a touch of kitsch here and there. Broken bottles and colourful glass marbles enhance the crumbling plaster walls, as do a few miscellaneous and appropriately tacky pictures. The mish-mash of Formica tables, comfortably worn armchairs and chilled soundtrack make it so inviting that you'll find no reason to leave before closing. The

friendly staff will happily make suggestions if you're at a loss as to which cocktail to order, and will put great care into preparing them, although it is equally a good place for beer. The inventive French menu is delicious and inexpensive, though you can always just settle for a plate of cheese or charcuterie. A room next to the bar, complete with sofa and board games, is reminiscent of an OAP's nest – great, if privacy is what you're after.

Kong, 1 rue du Pont Neuf, Palais Royal
Tel: 01 40 39 09 00 www.kong.fr
Open: noon–2am. Closed Sundays.

You'd think Hello Kitty and her friends came up with the design for Kong, not Philippe Starck. A 'pretty in pink' décor, with light-boxed posters of geishas and cool would-be Japanese pop stars, as well as rocking-chair seats on a pebble-print carpet, is finished off with Hello Kitty, Pokémon and Manga paraphernalia behind the bar. Arrive looking good, not only to impress the beautiful staff that look like they've just popped out of a Calvin Klein advert, but also to blend in with the Parisian yuppies who come here to flaunt their stuff. It's also popular

with Japanese tourists who'll come to snack on the delicious sushi. Located at the top of Kenzo's flagship store, it's a great place to have a cocktail at happy hour (6–8pm) after shopping around the Marais, and to watch the orange sun setting over the Seine – although the best views are from the restaurant upstairs, which, with its domed ceilings reminiscent of a botanical hothouse, is simply spectacular.

The Lounge Bar, Hotel Pershing Hall, 49 rue Pierre Charron, Champs-Élysées
Tel: 01 58 36 58 00 www.pershinghall.com
Open: 6pm–2am daily

Situated in the über-fashionable Hotel Pershing Hall located in near the swanky streets of Paris' 'golden triangle', the Lounge Bar is as decadent as it gets (and that's not just because of the cocktail prices). Classical high ceilings, complete with ornate covings, are teamed up with modern accessories:

ruby-red glass chandeliers; boxy chairs upholstered in grey, prune and chest-nut leather; string curtains illuminated with pink and blue lighting; and shelving displaying with red Murano glass vases (make sure you don't get too drunk and accidentally knock one over). The towering champagne-lined bar is magnificent, radiating a pink glow that makes you feel as if you're sitting in a champagne-filled aquarium. A trend-friendly crowd regularly check their appearance in the pink tinted mirrors on the way to the small mezzanine area, from which they survey fellow glamouristas swaying to the beats of the daily DJ. And you can nibble on a selection of Asian/sushi dishes right up until midnight.

Ourcq, 68 quai de la Loire, La Villette

Tel: 01 42 40 12 26   www.barourcq.com

Open: 3pm–midnight Wed–Thurs, Sun; 3pm–2am Fri–Sat

It's admittedly a little far off the beaten track, but this bar is a great find if you're spending the day at the MK2 canalside cinemas, or on your way back from the ultra-cool Villette complex. There is something of the original underground cyber-cafés of 1995 about this bar, with combat-trouser-wearing, tattooed trendies (who all look like web designers) fiddling with their iPods and Apple Macs in order to play their recently downloaded techno

through the sound system. You can follow suit, as there's free WiFi. The drinks are cheap, the atmosphere laid back and friendly. There's a comfy raised section behind the bar where it's easy to lose track of time, but it's outside (probably because Ourcq has a non-smoking policy) where the crowds gather. Amazingly, for such a small bar, famous DJs such as Princess Lea and Howie B come to play here.

La Palette, 43 rue de Seine, St Germain
Tel: 01 43 26 68 15
Open: 9am–2am Mon–Sat. Closed Sundays and throughout August.

Although you will find that an older clientele of gallery-owning types lunch on the plat de jour here during the day, La Palette is predominantly a bar. Scruffy students (the École des Beaux-Arts is just up the road) mingle with

well-heeled youngsters in this upmarket stretch of the Latin Quarter, to drink great wine, Ricard and Pernod, and create loud chatter and clouds of smoke. The back room, behind the traditional zinc bar, has a predominantly brown interior, with tiled murals, artworks and mirrors. But what people really come here for is the terrace located on the corner of the narrow rue de Seine that's able to accommodate a large number of tables (which quickly get taken up). The laid-back, al fresco feel offers a slice of Mediterranean life and comes into its own at night.

La Perle, 78 rue Vieille-du-Temple, Marais
Tel: 01 42 72 69 93
Open: 6am–2am Mon–Fri; 8am–2am Sat–Sun

Paris has its fair share of retro 1970s tabacs and bistros, demonstrating the fantastic versatility of Formica. What separates La Perle from all the others is its super-trendy crowd of fashionistas and models, beautiful staff, top-quality wine and lively house music. Come on a Sunday afternoon or early morning (at all other times it is packed, packed, packed), and you will be able to appreciate the amazingly kitsch retro décor of Formica orange-panelled walls, Formica veneered bar, and – you've guessed it – Formica cube tables.

There are bar stools along the bar as well as along one side of the window – great for people-watching (although it's entertaining enough inside), or there are diner-style booths at the back. The food isn't half bad if your stomach needs lining. In the summer, there's an Absolutely Fabulous terrace spilling out onto the quiet street of rue de la Perle and Vieille-du-Temple. Don't approach the terrace unless you're wearing sunglasses hot off the runway. Definitely one of the coolest spots in Paris.

Le Petit Fer à Cheval, 30 rue Vieille du Temple, Marais
Tel: 01 42 72 47 47 www.cafeine.com
Open: 9am–2am daily

Le Petit Fer à Cheval probably gets the prize for smallest bar in Paris, its central horseshoe bar from which it takes its name taking up all of the space at the front. It is otherwise decorated in typical Belle Époque style, and if you manage to squeeze past the crowd at the bar, under the impressive antique clock, you will find a more spacious back room with rail carriage-style wooden benches, a mosaic floor and Deconstructivist paintings of musical instruments on the walls. Traditional French food is on offer including huge and delicious salads. The outside terrace tables are like gold dust, but if you miraculously manage to bag yourself one (it's a good strategic manoeuvre to loiter around, secretly hawk-eyed, or to pretend to be

looking at your map outside), it's hard to beat the atmosphere created by being at the centre of the Marais' hustle and bustle.

Au P'tit Garage, 63 rue Jean-Pierre Timbaud, Oberkampf
Tel : 01 48 07 08 12
Open: 6pm–2am daily

There is something very 'Ost Berlin' about this bar, with its graffiti-covered loos, red and yellow flaking walls and mixed bag of cigarette-burnt Formica tables. An inexplicable 1950s retro fridge stands in one corner and a set of weighing scales lies abandoned on the floor… very conceptual. Dotted around are shelves with funky bric-à-brac, framed vintage magazine cut-outs

and posters of happening local music nights. The bar is made up of three rooms – what used to be a butcher's, a clothes shop and a garage, the last of these giving its name to the bar. A sign saying 'No table service' hangs on the wall, for the barman is far too busy trying to find the tune to match his mood – be it a grandiose Wagnerian bash or something more along the lines of Kraftwerk, you're guaranteed it'll be loud.

Pop In, 105 rue Amelot, Oberkampf

Tel: 01 48 05 56 11
Open: 6.30pm–1.30am. Closed Mondays, two weeks in December and August.

Very crowded, and very, very cool, this is one of the most popular bars in town. It's a favourite with the arty fringe, where boys sport tight black jeans and asymmetric hairstyles and girls paint their lips in retro red and curl their tinted hair. There's usually a crowd of them sitting on the pavement outside, taking regular intervals of fresh air from the smoky and packed rooms of Pop In (hence the name). The front door opens onto a small bar, which is very red and very crowded, beyond which is a narrow wooden staircase (watch out for the stumbling drunk) up to two packed rooms filled

with an assortment of tables separated by a very narrow, generally clogged corridor. Once you've managed to squeeze past this crowd, head down another very narrow staircase to a boxy underground room with an ever-flowing bar. Suddenly, you'll be dancing to funky electro-pop along with 50 other incredibly sweaty people, happily ignoring the dripping ceiling.

Le Pub Saint-Germain, 17 rue de l'Ancienne Comédie, St-Germain
Tel: 01 56 81 13 13
Open: 24 hours daily

More akin to a gastro-pub that a traditional British boozer, this is a huge space united by a brown and beige colour scheme. The long bar at the front has large, comfy brown leather sofas and a section of terracotta wall with sunflowers. The back, which leads to a quaint, cobbled street, is decorated in

a more sombre colonial style. An adjacent room has an Asian theme. None of this is really important, however, because at night it's so dark you can barely see anything at all – which hardly matters, as you're probably there on a blurry-visioned bender anyway, not to appreciate the décor. The food is uninspired, although good for emergency fuelling, so it's surprising to see Parisians coming here for lunch and ordering bottles of Jacob's Creek.

Le Rendezvous des Amis, 23 rue Gabrielle, Montmartre
Tel: 01 46 06 01 60   www.rdvdesamis.com
Open: 8.30am–2am daily

Aptly named, Le RDV des Amis was opened by six friends who wanted to create a social hub for Montmartre's young arty community. Indeed, everybody here seems to know one another, and there is a lot of table-hopping among the different groups. The vibe is so laid back that it's sometimes difficult to tell who is manning the bar – regulars often going behind it to serve themselves while the barman lounges at one of the tables. This laissez-faire attitude is also reflected in the décor: the ceilings are covered in photos of regulars and staff, and the interior is neglected except for the latest carefully hung temporary art exhibition. There's a second room at the back where

you can sometimes catch live bands – it's just like a student common room, centered round what looks like an IKEA sofa. It's student prices here too, with good wine and plates of cheese or charcuterie. Situated on the steep climb from Les Abbesses towards Sacré Coeur, it's the perfect place to get away from the suffocating swarms of map-folding tourists in the area.

Le Rubis, 10 rue du marché Saint-Honoré, Palais Royal
Tel: 01 42 61 03 34
Open: noon–10.30pm Mon–Fri. Closed Saturday evenings and Sunday.

Brimming with character, this tiny wine bar is located on the rue du marché Saint-Honoré. Its unadulterated 1950s interior reflects the loyalty of its regulars, who are drawn to the bar like bees to honey. While businessmen take over the banquettes at lunch for basic hearty food at cheap prices, a young, laid-back crowd flocks there in the evenings. Le Rubis focuses on Beaujolais and Loire wines. When the year's new Beaujolais Nouveau is released to the world on the third Thursday in November, the celebrations here spill out onto the street. Neither the wine nor the food will blow you away (although the unpretentious menus for both are a sure thing); nevertheless, Le Rubis has a certain je ne sais quoi that'll steal your heart away. Aperitifs are served with *coupelles de saucisson* on the upturned wine barrels outside,

come rain or shine.

The Bar, Le Plaza Athénée, 25 avenue Montaigne, Champs-Élysées

Tel: 01 53 67 66 00   www.plaza-athenee-paris.com

Open: 6pm–2am daily

The name may be simple but it's pretty accurate – the stylish and glamorous bar at the swanky Le Plaza Athénée hotel really is THE bar. Interior designer Patrick Jouin shows us just how well a classic interior can get a modern face-lift. The bar is divided into two areas. One is dominated by the long, blue, electrically illuminated bar made entirely of glass, complemented by high steel tables and stools, each set lit up with its own low-hung blue LED chandelier. The other has a lampshade larger than your bedroom which casts a warm, pink glow over low club chairs and tables. Dress up to join an

expensively heeled crowd, who sashay in to flaunt recent extravagances from Paris' most exclusive streets over delicious and innovative €25-a-pop cocktails (some of which turn up in lolly-form, part of a top-secret process of freezing alcohol) and top-quality bar snacks.

Wax, 15 rue Daval, Bastille
Tel: 01 40 21 16 16
Open: 9pm–5am Wed–Sun

Not quite a bar, not quite a club, Wax boasts that it is Paris' first 'DJ-bar'. If you like the 1970s, this is the place to be, since no effort has been spared in decking it out with retro furniture and light fittings. The psychedelic sea of purple, orange and chrome is initially a mild assault on the senses, but you

soon settle into the cool, laid-back surroundings. There are many discreet little seating areas where you can lounge with friends, as well as a medium-sized dance-floor to unwind those moves. The music is disco, of course – every night – but from a more original school than the ubiquitous Bee Gees or Weather Girls experience. And they do tend to throw in a bit of house music or R&B for variety.

Notes & Updates

snack...

Parisians like to stick to their regimented meal-times, and to take their time over three-course extravaganzas, so the concept of the snack hasn't fully been grasped. The number of slim silhouettes testifies that this is not a nation of grazers. It can be tricky trying to find a light lunch past 2pm unless you are either shopping in a department store (even they acknowledge the need for a snack to refuel energy reserves depleted by shopping) or in one of the more continental *quartiers*.

Retail eating is taken as seriously as everything else on sale. The Delicabar, with a fantastic roof-top courtyard, and Le Comptoir Picnic, in the mouth-watering Grande Epicerie (food hall), are just two of the four very hip places to eat in the Bon Marché. Printemps has a snack bar overseen by famous chef Alain Ducasse ('Be'), while Galeries Lafayette has its own branch of Maxim's, and Café Sushi, where you can feast not only on raw fish, but also on breathtaking views of the Opéra Garnier.

If you're exploring the city rather than the shops, then the Marais' Jewish quarter, around rue des Rosiers, offers fantastic falafel as well as kosher pizza around the clock, but keep some room for the poppy-seed cake at Korcarz. One can replenish with Middle-Eastern, syrup-soaked delights and savoury pies at the *salon de thé* in La Mosquée de Paris (see Eat) or La Bague de Kenza where rue Saint-Maur meets Oberkampf.

The only other source of round-the-clock sustenance are the brasseries, but the food served is rather unadventurous (basically the brasserie staples of *croque-monsieurs* and *madames*). For the ultimate hedonist's need for a snack, seek out the more glamorous brasseries with shellfish counters, such as Lutétia on boulevard Raspail or La Coupole on boulevard Montparnasse – you can't beat a plate of oysters *(huîtres)* washed down with a glass of champagne.

Tea and cake do not constitute meals. *L'heure du thé* (tea-time) is a different story altogether, and, for a nation of coffee drinkers, tea is taken very seriously, with some speciality tea shops (the highest concentration of which are on the

Left Bank) boasting over a 1,000 blends. All three Mariage Frères shops have a *salon de thé*, where you can have your cake and eat it. Long gone are the days when tea-time meant old doilies, chipped china and a token granny.

Cake destroyed the French monarchy after Marie Antoinette was maligned for trying to offer some to the poor, and Sofia Coppola's recent film about the misunderstood but rather hedonistic queen has put cake and pastel colours back on the post-ironic fashion map. Ladurée was the pastry consultant on the film, and this is the place to indulge your sweet cravings: it's been creating its world-famous macaroons since 1871. Pierre Hermé is another pâtissier of note; although neither of his two pâtisseries has a *salon de thé*, you can have his pasties for breakfast at Market (see Eat). This is not unusual: most cake shops do not do sit-down tea, which suggests that either cakes are a luxury to be brought and offered to friends as part of supper, or that Parisians prefer not to indulge in public. Du Pain et des Idées on the corner of rue Yves Toudic and rue de Marseille is ideally located for buying pastries to eat by the Canal Saint-Martin – you'll be able to smell the sweet brioche for miles, so let your nose guide you… Boulangerie Arnaud Delmontel on rue des Martyrs won the

'Croissant of the Year' award in 2006 (ah, to be on that panel of judges…) and, strangely, has collaborated with a hip graphic company 'Atomic Soda' to design the Hello Kitty-inspired 'Choco-Miss' cake.

In the summer months, Parisians like to picnic. In a city where most parks forbid you to sit on the grass, locals have reclaimed their urban environment. The banks of the river Seine, the canalside and the pedestrian Pont des Arts serve as concrete-stone spaces on which al fresco feasting is indulged in, from a simple baguette with goat's cheese to a lavish picnic of fois gras complete with bottles of wine. Eating on a blanket at any of these locations is a wonderful experience, and with Paris' large selection of delis, it's worth spending an evening joining the picnickers. If you're too lazy to put a picnic together, head to the Canal Saint-Martin's Pink Flamingo, which will deliver your pizza order to your chosen canalside spot.

Angelina's, 226 rue du Rivoli, Louvre/Palais Royal
Tel: 01 42 60 82 00
Open: 9am–7pm dialy

Located as it is, exactly halfway between the start of the Champs-Élysées and the Louvre, Café Angelina is never going to be a secret hideaway. As you enter through the colonnade opposite the Jardin des Tuileries, you find yourself at the front of the café – where a shop sells biscuits, jams and, of course, the ubiquitous pâtisserie. Further inside a large and ornate salle is painted in gold and decorated with huge murals and mirrors. Light streams

in from a skylight above. At the back a smaller, non-smoking room resounds to the click of expensive heels on parquet floor. Everything is charmingly worn, from the red carpet to the brown leather chairs and green marble tables, constantly occupied by a stream of hungry mouths. The waiters seem to enjoy playing up to the off-hand Parisian stereotype, even though, deep down, they are helpful and considerate. And then of course there is the reason you are there – the cakes. They might not be cheap, and you might have to queue for them, but they are well worth the wait.

Le Big Ben, Place Louis Armand, Gare de Lyon
Tel: 01 43 43 09 06 www.le-train-bleu.com
Open: 7:30am–11pm Mon–Fri; 9am–11pm Sat–Sun

Situated in the Gare de Lyon, this is a most unusual station buffet. A people-watching extravaganza, the café/bar is filled with quirky characters waiting for their trains, knitting or leisurely reading the paper while smoking

Gauloises. Furnished with dark burgundy armchairs, curtains and carpet, the long, and appropriately train-like corridor leads away from the historic Le Train Bleu restaurant.

An upmarket English breakfast is on offer here, along with its usual Continental counterpart, and delicious snacks in the form of salads, club sandwiches, quiches and pastas are served until 8.30pm. Brunch is reserved for Sundays and put on hold from July till September. The bar, needless to say, offers a comprehensive cocktail list. The grandeur and splendour of the bar and Salon de Thé have slightly decayed, and you can hear a distant echo of passing traffic and train announcements, but this only adds to the atmosphere, making you feel like the protagonist of a 1930s spy novel or film noir.

Café Le Basile, 34 rue Grenelle, St Germain
Tel: 01 42 22 59 46
Open: 7am–9.30pm Mon–Fri; 7.30am–8pm Sat. Closed Sundays.

When your feet are tired from shopping for fabulous footwear on rue Grenelle (Charles Jourdan at No. 17, Patrick Cox at No. 21) or if you'd

rather smell the scent of *croques* and coffee than designer perfumes (Frédéric Malle at No. 37), Café Le Basile is ideally placed. A glossy red and yellow Perspex bar sits at the front, where you perch on red-topped stools at high tables. Otherwise, at the back, where there's no shortage of space, red banquettes and white Formica tables look cool against a backdrop of 1950s retro prints. The open, sliding windows flood the space with natural light and keep the temperature comfortable during the summer. A huge colour photo of a young, pouting Mick Jagger mirrors the pouting Parisian clientele, although when it comes to finding anything to match the beautiful black-and-white print of a moody-looking Dylan at the back, we're stumped.

Café Beaubourg, 100 rue Saint-Martin, Beaubourg
Tel: 01 48 87 63 96
Open: 8am–1am (2am Fri–Sat) daily

Situated on the lively plaza in front of the Pompidou Centre, this café is popular with the iBook generation (there is free WiFi internet access). The huge terrace is a neat play on the traditional brasserie, with the usual rows of tables and chairs unusually made out of white steel and coloured plastic.

The modern design is beginning to look just a little faded, however – not surprisingly, given it dates from 1985. Inside the colour scheme is more subdued, with black chairs and white marble floors and tables, which only manages to avoid being austere through quirky pieces of art and book-shelves breaking up the wall space. A sweeping, polished concrete staircase leads to a second floor that is only open in exceptionally busy periods. The chilled atmosphere seems to be popular both with rich kids loudly drinking cocktails and more solitary aesthetes tapping away at their laptops. The salads in particular are excellent.

Café Fleurus, 2 rue de Fleurus, St Germain
Tel: 01 45 44 79 79
Open: 8am–6.30pm. Closed August.

One of the most stylish and funky tabac-cafés you'll find in Paris, Fleurus is light and airy, decorated with pink Perspex structures on the ceiling and monochrome harlequin screen-prints. A young crowd sits on banquettes at white Formica tables, served by old men who seem to have worked here for generations. It's a perfect place to breakfast or rest aching feet after

shopping at the APC fashion emporium opposite (see Shop), or for a fortify-ing perambulation in the nearby Jardin du Luxembourg. A simple menu of cheese plates, omelettes and sandwiches is on offer, and for breakfast there's the *pâtisserie du jour*, and, of course, as many cigarettes as you can smoke.

Cafés et Thés Verlet, 265 rue Saint-Honoré, Louvre
Tel: 01 42 60 67 39
Open: 9.30am–6.30pm. Closed Sundays.

A blissfully quiet experience – Verlet is set back only one road from the teeming rue du Rivoli. Boasting more than 100 varieties of tea and 30 types of coffee, the café is a temple to caffeine. Its altar consists of a dark wooden counter with shelf upon shelf of brown leaves, all packed in small, foil-lined, wooden crates that passed through the Suez Canal en route to your cup. The small (20 capacity) room downstairs is traditional – almost rustic – in style and bedecked with all manner of tea and coffee ephemera, while upstairs feels more contemporary, with a huge window at one end that's

perfect for people-watching. If the choice is a little overwhelming, the owner
– the excellent M Duchossoy – will be happy to guide customers through
his handpicked selection. And if you like what you try, you can buy a bag to
take home with you.

La Charlotte de l'Isle, 24 rue Saint-Louis-en-l'Île, Ile St-Luis
Tel: 01 43 54 25 83 www.la-charlotte.fr
Open: 2–8pm Thurs–Sun. Closed July and August.

A place of fairy-tales, magically conjured up by the eccentric *chocolatière* and
poetess, Madame Sylvie Langlet. Her tea shop La Charlotte de L'Isle is full to
the brim with witches on broomsticks, strange artefacts, tiny gnomes,

chocolate sculptures, carnival masks and marionettes (which come alive
during her puppet shows every Wednesday, by reservation only). A small
counter in the front room is where she's been serving her potent chocolate

for over 30 years, while a piano is the focus for her song and poetry readings every Friday from 6pm. At the back the few tightly squeezed tables are filled by those perusing the huge list of fragranced teas, although it's really the hot chocolate you should be having. What's more, she'll let you have a wander around her kitchen, where the magic happens and see all the guises her chocolate moulds come in! After indulging here you really feel you'll live happily ever after.

Chez Jeannette, 47 rue du Faubourg-Saint-Denis, Grands Boulevards
Tel: 01 47 70 30 89
Open: daily, 8am–8pm

Timeless, a neon tube light violently drilled into the elaborate cornicing, the decaying interior is reminiscent of cafés found today only in Havana or Bombay. And it is as shabby as the atmospheric street it's on, opposite Passage Brady, dominated by Indian restaurants. The action is centered

round a zinc bar, with colourful neon and a 'Chez Jeannette' sign overhead. A few booths lurk at the back of the L-shaped room, dotted with tables and surrounded by mirrors. Run by three busty and feisty ladies of a certain age – one dedicated to her small kitchenette behind the bar, the other two walking to and fro serving the swollen omelettes or fried chicken and potatoes feisty lady number one has just whisked up. Fellow diners include a contingent of arty hipsters and middle-aged scruffy flâneurs reading the papers and chain-smoking.

Colette Water Bar, 213 rue Saint-Honoré, Louvre
Tel: 01 55 35 33 90 www.colette.fr
Open: 11am–7pm daily

Here, in lifestyle concept store Colette's basement Water Bar, retail sluts collapse from nervous excitement at the beautifully laid-out designer must-haves upstairs. A large communal table and two rows of smaller tables are lit by strong halogen lights hanging low from red cords, illuminating the cool blue drinking glasses and orchids. As it is a 'water bar', rows of plastic water

bottles line the back of the bar, facing the funky neon-lit illustration hanging on the wall. For the discerning water connoisseur 73 different brands are on offer, including the overpriced 'Bling', whose bottle has been customized with Swarovski crystals. Four Coca-Cola fridges (the more brands on show, the merrier) contain a choice of detox energy drinks, beers and designer smoothies. In keeping with the variety of brands stocked both in the shop and bar, the menu – which changes daily – is largely imported from other 'designer' eateries; the salads come from the Rose Bakery and the cakes from Ladurée.

Le Confiturier, 20 rue du Cherche-Midi, St-Germain
Tel: 01 45 49 33 64
Open: 8am–6.30pm. Closed Sundays.

As its name suggests, this café specializes in stylishly presented breakfasts, offering a variety of loose-leaf teas from Le Palais des Thés as well as the more ubiquitous café and croissant. The emphasis is on quality rather than quantity. A selection of cakes, delicious home-made crumbles and scones waits expectantly for the afternoon crowd. The décor is the unlikely mix of

modern minimal-ism, rustic kitchen and colonial safari (that'll be the leopard-printed seat cushions), but works largely due to the personal and homely vibe created by the friendly couple who run it. Chic Parisiennes with discerning palates come here when shopping in the area.

La Contrescarpe, 57 rue Lacépède, Latin Quarter
Tel: 01 43 36 82 88
Open: daily, 7am–2am

Apart from the fabulously spacious terrace overlooking the picturesque square of Place de la Contrescarpe, where jazz is sometimes performed during the summer, La Contrescarpe is nothing special on the outside. Once

inside, however, three distinct seating areas are available to choose from: the front cosy library, with dark walnut bookshelves, green walls and benches, and brown, soft leather club chairs; the light dining room, with pale wicker chairs, off which is hidden a discreet drinking den, with low, cushioned seating and tables; and, finally, a delightful little patio with generously spaced tables and bushy plants. Locals devour the bargain menus (lunch €15, dinner €24) of bistro-style food (fantastic *poulet rôti avec frîtes*), while students spend hours chatting away in a smoke-filled corner, lounging on leather banquettes.

La Galerie des Gobelins, Hôtel Plaza Athénée, 25 avenue Montaigne, Champs-Élysées
Tel: 01 53 67 66 65 www.plaza-athenee-paris.com
Open: 8am–1am daily

The Plaza Athénée's resident pastry chef Christophe Michalak's delicious creations are worth a trip to the hotel even if you can't afford to shop round here. You won't find a more learned pastry genius than Michalak, who previously worked for Ladurée and Pierre Hermé, and was captain to the team that won the World Pastry Cup in 2005 (yes, there is such a trophy) –

they so impressed President Chirac that they were awarded a Sèvres vase! Michalak's cakes are like beautiful works of art with an avant-garde take on the traditional: profiteroles served on spikes and spiked with ginger, peanut butter macaroons. And if you haven't got a sweet tooth, try one of the quadruple-decked club sandwiches on offer. Classical columns and neo-classical furnishings decorate the long gallery lined with vast crystal chandeliers, and the immense windows opening onto the beautiful courtyard are dressed with warm, orangey-red silk curtains – all presided over by the sound of a harp or piano.

Ladurée, 75 avenue des Champs-Élysées, Champs-Élysées
Tel : 01 40 75 08 75 www.laduree.fr
Open: 7.30am–11pm daily

There are three Ladurée tea houses in Paris and the one thing they all have in common is the long counter, lit with neo-classical statuettes holding lampshades, which is home to a technicolour dream of the creamy delights

and macaroons for which Ladurée is famous. The original tea room (and the most basic in décor), opened in 1862 on 16 rue Royale, is said to be the first of its kind in Paris; the other two are modern additions carefully craft-ed to replicate the style of the first. The Champs-Élysées branch is the biggest and the grandest. Upstairs is pure opulence: a light and airy baby blue room is complete with grandfather clock, candelabra, chandeliers and gilt mirrors. A darker, chinoiserie-styled central room, a small mock library and two further dining rooms all exude luxury. They are interconnected by way of a long, creaky, wooden-floored corridor, leading finally to the plush bathrooms. The more dressed-down extension at the front allows cus-tomers to idly watch passers-by shop in the Champs-Élysées. A place to soak up pre-revolutionary grandeur.

Lô Sushi, 8 rue de Berri, Champs-Élysées
Tel: 01 45 62 01 00
Open: noon–12:30am daily

Business lunchers and shoppers perch beside the bar of this conveyer-belt sushi restaurant just off the Champs-Élysées. It follows the now well-known formula: watch the sushi pass by and pick up the ones you like the look of, priced according to the colour of the plates, while a smiley waitress is summoned to serve drinks. The space, designed by Andrée Putman, is large and airy, with flat-screen TV monitors distracting diners with flashing film

clips, while funky music pumps out of discreet white speakers. The high-quality sushi rotates around the clock from noon to midnight, although the atmosphere is buzziest around lunchtime. Take care not to use the small square dish on the counter for soy sauce and wasabi – it's an ashtray.

Le Loir dans la Théière, 3 rue des Rosiers, Marais
Tel: 01 42 72 90 61
Open: 11.30am–7pm Mon–Fri; 10am–7pm Sat–Sun

On the edge of the edgy Marais, this coffee shop is always full of bright young things discussing their plans for the evening or the events of the night before. The two large inter-connecting rooms, deliberately bohemian

and ramshackle, are covered with layer upon layer of old show posters and mismatched furniture, while all available shelf-space is taken up by quirky bric-à-brac. The friendly atmosphere is laid-back to the point where it can be difficult to tell the casually dressed waiters from the customers. Excellent home-made cakes are washed down with a choice from 18 types of tea. Alcohol and light meals can also be ordered if you find that you've settled in and don't want to leave just yet in pursuit of the evening plan.

Mamie Gateaux, 66 rue du Cherche-Midi, St Germain
Tel: 01 42 22 32 15
Open: 11.30am–6pm. Closed Sundays and Mondays.

One would be forgiven for thinking that Mamie Gateaux was the principal character of a series of books or films set in this café. It's a nostalgic and loving recreation of a rapidly disappearing style of Frenchness, with furnishings from the 1930s to the '50s, which only a foreigner could have thought up. That foreigner is the Japanese owner, who has also opened the Brocante a few doors down and is planning to open a drapery store, all in line with

this particular aesthetic, which is reminiscent of the Truffaut era. The menu, a simple sheet of paper printed to look like a leaf out of an écolier's home-work book, features brioche, soups, quiches, salads and cakes, catering for elevenses, light lunches and teas, all in line with school breaks, but without the screaming children.

Mariage Frères, 30 and 35 rue du Bourg Tibourg, Marais
Tel: 01 42 72 28 11
Open: 10.30am–7pm daily

France's first importer of tea (1660) opened its original teahouse and shop on the narrow Marais street Du Bourg Tibourg in 1854, and has been serving chic Parisians ever since. Serious tea-lovers frequent Mariage Frères, not

only to sit in the colonial-styled tearoom, but also to buy the exquisite tea to take home. Staff sport white linen suits, reminiscent of the undyed muslin sacks that form the elegant Mariage Frères tea bags. But if you're after loose leaves, hundreds of black tea cans line the oak shelves and you can lean over the counter and stick your nose into each and every one of them (time and patience permitting). The salon offers the same huge selection of tea, as well as tea-scented cakes, light snacks and salads. Two other tea rooms have opened (13 rue des Grands Augustins, tel: 01 40 51 82 50) and (260 Faubourg Saint-Honoré, tel: 01 46 22 18 54).

Pink Flamingo, 67 rue Bichat, Canal St Martin
01 42 02 31 70
Open: noon–3pm, 7–11pm Tues–Fri; 4–11.30pm Sat–Sun

A stone's throw from the St-Martin canal, Pink Flamingo has had the novel idea of the 'pink-nik'. After ordering your pizza, you're given a balloon (so they can recognize you) and off you go to find an idyllic spot by the waterside where they'll deliver it. If the 'pink-nik' isn't permitted by the weather, they do have a small inside space next to the counter and kitchen. This isn't

your average pizzeria: unusual ingredients such as figs and hummus appear
on pizzas named after unusual idols such as 'La Bjork' and 'Le Basquiat'.
What's more, the thin bases are made with organic flour and virgin olive oil.
The funky décor has a black and pink painted exterior with a pink flamingo
sign and *la salle d'à côté* is filled with garden furniture covered in plastic chequered tablecloths. Jugs of water with fluorescent plastic cups sit by the
window beside club flyers left to find their way to the trendy clientele.

Aux Pipalottes Gourmandes, 49 rue Rochechouart, Montmartre
Tel: 01 44 53 04 53
Open: 10am–10pm daily

The number of delis and traiteurs on Paris' streets, all with exquisitely
arranged plates of mouth-watering food in their windows, is simply amazing.

The problem is where to eat it: cart it back to the hotel (by which time your food lust will have subsided), or eat it on a park bench (not great in winter)? What's really needed is a couple of tables where you can sample the displayed delights. Aux Pipalottes Gourmandes has just that. Four tables sit at the centre of this deli, surrounded by shelves piled high with produce, the deli counter at the front's selection of dishes ranges from stuffed peppers to home-made gnocchi and foie gras. Parisian locals devour everything washed down with bottles of carefully acquired wine (it's so popular you can even book). Mariage Frères teas and freshly ground coffee complement the excellent cake. Foodies be warned: it's almost impossible to resist buying the entire content of the shop on your way out.

Poilâne, 8 rue du Cherche-Midi, St Germain-des-Prés
Tel: 01 45 48 42 59 www.poilane.fr
Open: 7.15am–8.15pm daily

There aren't many breads like Poilâne: brown, dense and chewy, with a dark burnt crust full of flavour – almost certainly best toasted. And there certainly aren't many breads as famous as Poilâne. It's flown all over the world (they have even built a bakery near the airport to meet the demand), and

with a bakery and shop now in London, which distributes to exclusive London delis, the Poilâne phenomenon is international. It's still run by the Poilâne family, who started the business in the 1930s, and the philosophy behind the success is teaming traditional recipes with modern marketing – what the late Lionel Poilâne liked to call his 'retro-innovation'. If you're already a fan of his famous bread, it is certainly worth making the pilgrimage to the original shop, decked out in wood, with rows of the flour-powdered dome-shaped loaves served in quarters, halves or wholes by a dozen ladies in white pinafores.

Pozzetto – Caffè Gelato, 39 rue du Roi de Sicile, Marais
Tel: 01 42 77 08 64 www.pozzetto.biz
Open: noon–midnight daily

A surprisingly skinny man (how doesn't he give in to the temptation?) will serve you 'heaven on a cone' in this *caffè gelato* in the Marais. Parisians in

the know will tell you that neither Amorino, nor their native Berthillon (their rivalry always a topic of much debate), but Pozzetto serves up the best ice cream in Paris, possibly the world. The shop's mod-

ern, minimalist design, painted all-white, houses the freshly made ice cream in smallish stainless steel tubs. If ice cream isn't your thing try the coffee, which is amazing, as is the best chocolate spread in town. Open late, it's great for those 'I've had too many to care about my diet' moments.

Renoma Café Gallery, 32 avenue George V, Champs-Élysées
Tel: 01 47 20 46 19
Open: 8.30am–midnight daily

Unusual black-and-white photographs of models with montaged animal heads printed onto jazzed-up Louis XVI chairs complement the grey, black and white interior of Renoma Café Gallery. Otherwise, the space has a quasi-industrial feel to it with tubular ventilation pipes on show, white paint-ed brick walls and a concrete floor. Local fashionistas descend on Renoma

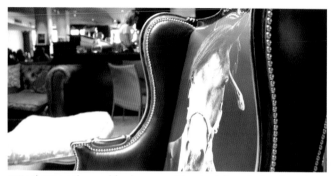

not only to eat the good food – reasonably priced given the location – but also to sip aperitifs after work, or while poring over the negs of the latest fashion shoot. From 3pm to midnight there's a limited menu for those who find themselves peckish between Paris' strict meal times, and a small table is laid out with Italian-style *aperitivo*, for those feeling the cocktails going to their head too quickly. Turntables and a projector in the corner suggest a clubbier vibe in the evenings.

Rose Bakery, 46 rue des Martyrs, Montmartre
Tel: 01 42 82 12 80
Open: 9am–7pm Tues–Sat; 10am–5pm Sun. Closed two weeks in August.

A piece of London in Paris, the Rose Bakery is for those who can't stomach another croissant or steak tartar. Opened by the husband and wife team (he's French, she's British) behind Villandry and the Rose Bakery in Dover

Street Market, London, it's a minimal affair; the converted *chartil* (where produce-sellers stored their food and veggie carts) has bare concrete floors, metal table-tops and a stainless-steel counter. Dishes of cabbage salads, marinated cucumbers, pies and mini pizzas are laid out near the entrance, while shelves display quintessentially British products (baked beans, Marmite, oatmeal crackers, cereal, tea, parsnip chips, etc.). Tea-time is an equally British affair involving carrot cake, shortbread, scones and English tea served in hippie earthenware. The brunch is a treat, with cooked servings of eggs, bacon, tomato and toast, or boiled eggs with Marmite toast, or porridge. A real success for Anglo–Franco relations – the locals love it!

Sand Set 36, 36 rue du Mont Thabor, Louvre
Tel: 01 42 96 01 31
Open: 8am–6pm. Closed Sundays.

Visitors to Paris will undoubtedly think the rise in the 'on the go' sandwich bars a shame (Parisians seem to treat them much like a novelty fashion item imported from New York); but sometimes, particularly when you don't want

to take much time off from shopping, they are super-handy to have around. Especially here, behind the rue de Rivoli and Tuileries (where you can 'take-out' and picnic), or off the exclusive shopping streets surrounding place Vendôme, where you'd otherwise pay outrageously inflated prices to sit down in a 'proper' café. A menu typical of its ubiquitous Anglo-Saxon counterpart offers pasta salads, toasted sandwiches and chocolate brownies, as well as a selection of French quiches, salads and macaroons. Orange-coloured Perspex chairs, high white designer stools, mirrors and black chandeliers show an awareness of a modern design ethic. Let's just hope it doesn't herald an end to the three-course lunch menu.

Thé-Troc, 52 rue Jean-Pierre-Timbaud, Oberkampf
Tel: 01 43 55 54 80
Open: 11am–6.30pm daily

Thé-Troc is one of the few remaining grungy establishments of the 11th arrondissement (along with the anti-globalisation, association-run, wholefood café La Passerelle (3 rue Saint-Hubert, tel: 01 43 57 04 82, www.ala-passerelle.org). It's a strange mix of ancient teahouse, comic-book shop and hippy-trippy store (the kind that sells smoking paraphernalia – though strangely, the café is non-smoking). To the right of the entrance is the shop, to the left the tearoom. An assortment of old wooden (and very narrow)

tables and stripy cushioned benches give the place true character. The walls are covered with ethnic craftwork (masks mainly), which are for sale, along with psychedelic posters of past rock concerts and drawings of spliff-smoking comic-book heroes. There are at least 100 different flavours of tea to choose from and, on a good day, their friends will pop in to serve you cake.

Notes & Updates

party...

Paris is not one of the cities that leaps to mind when doing a mental search of the world's best clubbing; nor is it locally or internationally renowned for the latest avant-garde music. London or New York purists would be horrified by the Parisian DJ habit of jumping genres indiscriminately, throwing in Madonna or The Cure during a techno set. Something else to be aware of is that club nights usually kick off with a live band, so don't leave before the DJ starts, thinking you're in the wrong joint.

Parisians go clubbing for a fun night out rather than for grooving to particular sounds of music or for trailing particular DJs. Also, as bars stay open till at least 2am, clubs will only get going at around 3am. But, although the music might fall short of more serious clubbers' tastes, the crowd's fun-loving, up-for-it attitude is infectious enough to carry you through any 1980s medley. And the clubs do attract some famous international DJs, while also having managed to export a funky French House scene led by the likes of Daft Punk, Cassius and Dimitri from Paris.

There are clubs to suit every predilection, from stadium-size Euro-trash clubs complete with laser shows, to smoother boutique clubs with sophisticated animations. Star DJs such as Paul van Dyke and Pete Tong headline at the former – these places will usually ask for a substantial entrance fee (around €20), though this often includes a 'conso' that buys you a free

drink. Le Pulp and Le Triptyque fall into the cooler, and slightly cheaper category (€10 entry); Ivan Smagghe, DJ at Le Pulp, hosts a night called 'Kill the DJ', whose fame has even reached London.

Parallel to this spectrum lies another that ranges from the grungy (such as Glaz'art, with its dreadlocked regulars) to the glitzy, located in the 'golden triangle' (such as Neo) and frequented by overripe sugar daddies with their model girlfriends. The glitzy clubs pride themselves on their 'select' door policy, making a sport of turning people away. Le Paris, Paris and Le Baron are the clubs of the moment, and getting into either of them requires strategic planning, a cool wardrobe and possibly a friend on the inside.

The indie rock scene is small and nothing like those of London and New York (this isn't surprising for a nation that still reveres Johnny Hallyday), though La Flèche d'Or, Le Truskel, Point Éphémère and Nouveau Casino are good venues to check out. For truly underground clubbing (quite literally), illegal parties take place in Paris's catacombs tunnelled beneath the streets, although these are becoming rarer due to police clampdowns (for more info, check out www.frotteconnard.tk).

Gay nights are well served in Paris, with most clubs offering at least one a week. Les Bains and Queen are perhaps the most famous, while the Sunday afternoon transsexual tea dance at Folie's Pigalle is great fun. Most clubs open at midnight and close at '*l'aube*' (dawn), although it's possible to keep going around the clock with the many 'after' parties (usually at weekends, and often gay) that start in the morning and continue through to the afternoon the next day.

Le Baron, 6 avenue Marceau, Trocadero

Tel: 01 47 20 04 01   www.clublebaron.com

Open: 11.30pm–late daily

The fantastically seedy décor of this former brothel has been left untouched. Posters from the 1920s picturing cavorting, semi-naked ladies, illuminated by a red glow from the tasselled lamps, hang above sexy red couches and candle-lit round tables. Be warned that these are more or less reserved for the regular champagne-guzzling VIPs, so you will be forced onto the very small and packed dance-floor. Unusually for the smaller Parisian

clubs, it's party time here every night of the week, with Mondays just as riotous as Saturday nights. Music Thursday to Saturday is always provided by a DJ, but you're likely to catch a live band as well on other nights. Run by the same team as Le Paris, Paris, this is considered to be one of the coolest nightspots in the city. With a door policy that Parisians call 'select', it's very difficult to get in, so make sure you're dressed to impress and that you've got Plan B already up your Gucci sleeve.

Le Bataclan, 50 boulevard Voltaire, Oberkampf

Tel: 01 43 14 00 30   www.le-bataclan.com

Open: 11.30pm–6am

Le Bataclan is famed for its legendary live music line-ups (previous acts include Lou Reed and Morcheeba), but occasionally at weekends they stage club nights that span a broad spectrum of music, from funk to techno to house. A converted theatre, the venue is immense, with a stage up front facing a space kitted out with tables and chairs, cabaret style. The remaining area has been transformed into a huge dance floor, where people dance or just stand, drinks in hand, chatting. During gigs it'll be rammed, but although

the club nights are harder to fill, there's enough of a crowd to give off a good party vibe – and what's more, you actually get space to dance! Cigarette ladies in costume, with hat and tray, add to the cabaret feel, and the mixed crowd reflects the mixed bag of tunes.

Batofar, opposite 11 quai Francois-Mauriac, Bercy
Tel: 01 53 60 17 30 www.batofar.org
Open: 11pm–6am Mon–Sat; 6am–noon, first Sunday of the month

There is something of the surreal world of *The City of Lost Children* aboard the club boat *Batofar* (one just wishes everyone were forced to wear the Jean-Paul Gaultier costumes). It's as if you've entered the depths of some-

one's dark imagination: you'll chance upon endless nooks and crannies to keep you entertained until the place starts to truly kick off, at around 3am. Be warned that the constricted space and the tiny circular windows mean a lack of proper ventilation, so it does get extremely hot! But that's a small price to pay for the pleasure of downing a beer while watching clueless fish swimming in the circular tank at the centre of the lounge area. A DJ stage lurks in the boat's main hold, where live bands appear at least once a week. Watch out for the quayside summer events where drinkers party on deck, as well as the morning revelry on the first Sunday of every month.

Cabaret 'Cab', 2 place du Palais Royal, Louvre
Tel: 01 58 62 56 25 www.cabaret.fr
Open: 6.30pm–dawn (2am Tues). Closed Sundays and Mondays.

Cabaret, otherwise know as the 'Cab', is probably the best-looking club in Paris (Ora-ito-designed). The space is huge and labyrinthine, with a myriad interconnecting rooms and dead-ends that all look a bit too similar in the dark red light, so take a ball of thread with you. Separating the restaurant from the club area is a large dance-floor that's illuminated by red strip lights on the floor, and is surrounded by bench-lined booths. Two separate rooms

have long rows of sexy red benches, each with its own oversized lampshade; another area has tables recessed into the ground, encircled with a tyre-like cushion so that you need to climb into them; there are two bars (or is it three?), and even a blue-lit aquarium. On Mondays and Tuesdays most of the areas are closed off and the space becomes more like an intimate DJ bar.

From Wednesday to Saturday, it's a proper club, drawing in glamorous crowds (especially Friday when it's 1980s Mania and Saturday when it's house).

Chez Carmen, 53 rue Vivienne, Grands Boulevards
Tel: 01 42 36 45 41
Open: midnight–9am Mon–Fri; midnight–noon Sat

The décor of this bar-cum-club is nothing spectacular, simply a square, mirrored room with a bar to one side. But at four in the morning (don't come here before then) it'll be so packed and you'll be so drunk that you simply

won't care. Loud house music is played to a crowd still merry from whichever club they've just been chucked out of. They don't want to go home, they want to party hard – and they can do it here, until the last person either leaves or falls over. Perfect for insomniacs or those with an early-morning Eurostar to catch. You won't remember getting here or leaving, but you'll have a feeling that you've just done something fun.

Le Divan du Monde, 75 rue des Martyres, Montmartre
Tel: 01 40 05 06 99 www.divandumonde.com
Open: 11.30pm–6am Fri–Sat (check website for weekday openings)

Club, bar, concert venue and art gallery, Le Divan du Monde attempts to be all things to all men and, remarkably, succeeds. The main space of this former theatre is usually home to installations by experimental artists, the aim

being to bring the work and public closer together. Around the installations they have gigs three times a week with music ranging from avant-garde electronica to traditional Armenian. Check the website first. From 11pm onwards, the main space is usually closed and the more intimate upstairs bar area (technically called 'Le Divan Japonais') opens. Entrance is free and its organically designed surroundings are an ideal place to kick back with friends and listen to some experimental electronica. Once a week the two floors are opened at the same time to create a club for 500 people. The baroque décor of the theatre and the more modern balcony area mesh together well, and these nights are filled with a young happy crowd dancing, drinking and flirting to music you will be familiar with.

Le Duplex, 25 rue Michel-le-Comte, Marais
Tel: 01 42 72 80 86
Open: 8pm–2am daily

If you're a gay man in Paris, be sure to stop off at Le Duplex. It's a rather shabby-chic bar with high ceilings and walls decked out with temporary art exhibitions. Predominantly

good-looking young men perch on high stools and tables near the bar, while the rest of the floor is kept empty to accommodate the crowds. There's proper seating upstairs on the mezzanine where the décor is more Berliner than Parisian. On Friday nights and throughout the weekend Duplex is full to the brim with a cruising crowd of party boys.

La Flèche d'Or, 102 bis rue de Bagnolet, Belleville
Tel: 01 44 64 01 02 www.flechedor.fr
Open: 8pm–5am (2am Sun–Mon). Closed Tuesdays.

This place is probably as close to London trendy as Paris deigns to come. It's located in the fashionable 20th in an abandoned metro station, and its interior was converted by students from the Beaux-Arts. The music, generally guitar-based indie and rock, is a welcome relief from the thumping dance

beats that prevail in the rest of the city. Concerts take place every night at La Flèche d'Or, which opens its doors from 8pm, and transforms into a club at about 11.30pm. The pleasantly shambolic interior is dominated by a model tube train crashing through the ceiling above the bar. Entry is free and they serve food (home-cooked style) until 1am in a small restaurant area off the main room. The crowd is laid back, but one word of warning: the bouncers have a bit of a reputation, so it's probably best to behave in the queue.

Folie's Pigalle, 11 place Pigalle, Pigalle

Tel: 01 48 78 55 25 www.folies-pigalle.com

Open: midnight–6am (11am Sat–Sun) daily

House, house, and more house. That just about describes the music policy of this famous *bôite*, which attracts the top stars of its chosen genre. But while the DJs may not vary the style much, the clientele could not be more diverse. This former strip-tease theatre is not for the faint-hearted, since it is almost guaranteed to be rammed, sweaty and very loud. Everything here is unapologetically brash and decadent, down to the red velour banquettes and golden scrolling of the main room. An air-conditioned balcony overlook-

ing the dance-floor is a welcome relief, for here things are a little calmer (but not much). At weekends the party goes on until 11am, and on Sunday afternoons there's 'La Gay Tea Dance', while Sunday night hosts Paris' biggest transsexual night. It's not that cheap (€20 entry for a start) but if you head out with an open mind and an open wallet you should have a raw, vicious night.

Glaz'art, 7–15 avenue de la Porte de la Villette, La Villette

Tel: 01 40 36 55 65 www.glazart.com

Open: 8pm–midnight Thurs; 6pm–6am Fri–Sat

Always an art gallery, sometimes a concert venue or club, Glaz'art caters for every musical taste from reggae and dub through to rock, jungle and techno. Only 100 metres from the city limits and the start of the infamous ban-lieues, the club attracts a friendly mix of unfussy people who arrive from all over Paris. It was formerly a bus station and the exterior is a little drab, but inside it feels more like someone's house, with armchairs and tables strewn around the large dance-floor. The club nights, which fittingly have a house-

party feel to them, get packed and sweaty, and the outside terrace provides some respite on hot summer nights. The next door car park is transformed into a rather trippy 'Alice in Wonderland on the Beach' themed funfair in the summer, which might explain the mystery of the sand in your shoes. Such an initiative is typical of Glaz'art's perception of its role as a venue, where you feel fun is more important than profit.

Man de la Ray, 32–34 rue Marbeuf, Champs-Élysées
Tel: 01 56 88 36 36 www.mandelaray.com
Open: 6pm–2am (6am Fri–Sat) daily

Le Man Ray was the place to see and be seen in when it was first opened in 1999 by Thierry Kléméniuk and celebs Johnny Depp, Sean Penn, Mick Hucknall and John Malkovich. The novelty has worn off a bit and the name slightly changed, but still it attracts a model crowd typical of the 8th arrondissement. The two-tiered space is enormous. The mezzanine bar, decorated with Man Ray's photographs, looks down onto the pan-Asian themed restaurant below. At the stroke of midnight the tables are cleared away to make room for the dance-floor and a curtain is pulled back to reveal a DJ booth decorated with wooden devil-like monsters (Friday and Saturday only). Among the usual popular 1980s and '90s revival nights, a few good DJs play (such as Kerri Chandler) and quality record labels (such as Defected) put on awesome nights. Although the food is an afterthought,

booking for dinner might be a way of securing entry into the club, which is otherwise barricaded by a row of beefy bouncers.

Mix Club, 24 rue de l'Arrivée, St Germain-des-Pres
Tel: 01 56 80 37 37 www.mixclub.fr
Open: midnight–6am Thurs–Sat; 5pm–1am Sun

A fairly serious and flashy house music club, popular with a young and excitable crowd, Mix attracts international Djs, and the Ministry of Sound put on regular nights here. Although it's housed in a basement, the ceilings are high enough to stop you from feeling suffocated, even when the club is full to bursting. There are three balconies from which you can observe the mayhem on the dance-floor, and the DJ booth is covered in hundreds of little LCD screens in case the music is not electronic enough for your taste. The impressively synchronized sound and light systems are given an extra

Ibiza vibe by a machine spewing out confetti at regular intervals. Outside there can be long queues, at the head of which the bouncers have been known to be obstructive, especially if you are a male-only group. On Thursdays foreigners get in for free before midnight, while Sunday is more of a gay night.

Nouveau Casino, 109 rue Oberkampf, Oberkampf

Tel: 01 43 57 57 40 www.nouveaucasino.net
Open: midnight–6am (Gigs start at 7pm – check website for listings)

Having experienced long-term success with their café-bar Café Charbon (see Drink), the team decided to convert the old factory space next door into a concert venue/club in 2001. Monday to Wednesday nights are reserved for gigs, ranging from pop-folk bands to the harder heavy. Fridays

and Saturdays, things get clubbier, with anything from a scratch massive to minimal Berliner techno. Thursday nights swing either way. Ornate chandeliers and a long illuminated red fibreglass bar contrast with the otherwise stark dance-floor and industrial interior. A chill-out mezzanine area behind the sound desk is filled with deep sofas for the over-worked and underwatered. The venture is another success for the crew, retaining the faithfully cool Charbon clientele, who invariably end up stumbling in from the bar once they've had a few too many, as well as gaining a new breed of acolytes who take their music seriously.

L'Opa, 9 rue Biscornet, Bastille

Tel: 01 46 28 12 90 www.opa-paris.com

Open: 8pm–2am Tues–Wed; 8pm–3am Thurs; 9pm–6am Fri–Sat. Closed throughout August.

This two-level warehouse space just behind the Bastille is host to an amalgamation of tech-media. You can sip a cocktail to urban jazz, nod intellectually to neo-folk, be entranced by video-art projections accompanied by electro-soundscapes, or simply have a fit on the dance-floor to

pumping techno. It just depends on what night you go on. Orange and blue water-filled lamps hang over the concrete bar, which is tended by a friendly, laid-back staff. Red stage lights illuminate the bare brick walls and the cocktail-list blackboards. White blinds come down over the large industrial windows and double up as screens for the well-crafted club visuals. In the early evening L'Opa is more of a bar, when trendy 20-somethings come to sit at the shiny copper octagonal tables, but slips into club mould as an (ever so slightly) older crowd joins the dance-floor. Upstairs is a further bar, decked out in bathroom tiles, with more space and tables where the partied-out 30-somethings can watch their young friends party on down below.

Le Paris, Paris, 5 avenue de L'Opéra, Louvre

Tel: n/a www.leparisparis.com

Open: midnight–6am Wed–Sat

Parisians describe 'Paris, Paris', along with its sister club Le Baron (in the 8th), as a club 'for beautiful people', a phrase they say in English. The tiny

space quickly fills up with a stunning crowd up for partying hard and fast (it's a full-blown party here by midnight, something you won't experience in other Parisian clubs), but if the 'beautiful' scene is not your thing, don't let that put you off – the quality music and potent cocktails are what you should come for. There's a tiny stage for the indie rock nights, which eventually gets swallowed up by the growing crowd as the bands retire and DJs take over. To get hassle-free entry (the bouncers seem to revel in turning people away), visit the website and sort out a guestlist through Marco (marco@leparisparis.com), informing him of the night you'd like to go to and the number of people you're bringing.

Point Éphémère, 200 quai de Valmy, Canal St Martin

Tel: 01 40 34 02 48 www.pointephemere.org
Open: midday–2am Mon–Sat, 1–9pm Sun

Basically, Point Éphémère is one large concrete box where a lot of really cool things happen. It could be a skinhead punk singing along to some funky techno. It could be an exhibition or a ballet. It could be a DJ competition. Whatever it is, this multimedia collective (there are artists' studios, recording studios, workshops, etc.) will attract an audience of 10th arrondissement hipsters. Matt steel tables are decked out with orange plastic chairs (like the ones you get in school canteens) and you can eat in the very brightly lit restaurant (make sure you're wearing tinted moisturiser), which is cornered off from the bar by a predominantly glass wall. Run by a non-profit-making organization committed to transforming industrial wastelands into creative centres, the landscape is undeniably urban: you can see the metro trains rolling past on the other side of the canal. The bar's big windows overlook

the cobbles of the atmospheric canalside space, which is a good place to
congregate, clutching pints of beer, when the inside's a little too packed.

Pulp, 25 boulevard Poissonnière, Grands Boulevards
Tel: 01 40 26 01 93 www.pulp-paris.com
Open: midnight–5am Wed–Sat

At the weekend it's a club for girls who like girls, but during the week a
mixed hip crowd come to enjoy one of the best DJ line-ups in town. Check
out the undeniably hip website, with its graphic illustrations and animated
flyers, for the programme. Funky house night 'Kill The DJ'
(www.killthedj.com), run by local Parisian hero DJ Ivan Smagghe, features
big-name DJs such as Andrew Weatherhall, who keep the young and the
wasted glued to the dance-floor until dawn (thus the bar is never too
crowded). Strangely during the day and early evening it doubles up as a ball-

room-dancing club for the (much) older generation who dress up à la Strictly Come Dancing… join in, or get a glimpse of them waiting for the club to open at around 3pm.

Queen, 102 avenue des Champs-Élysées, Champs-Élysées
Tel: 08 92 70 73 30   www.queen.fr
Open: 11.30pm–late daily

Famous for its long-running Sunday gay night 'Overkitsch', which regularly features fabulously camp acts including transsexual Eurovision hopeful Dana International, the appropriately named Queen is hand-on-knee gay-friendly every night. Otherwise, its accessible location, bang on the Champs-Elysées,

attracts people of all shapes and sizes, ages and persuasions. Monday is disco night, although you'd be forgiven for thinking it was a school disco given the large number of under-aged kids parading on the dance-floor (well, the ones that manage to fake it past the bouncer at any rate). Tuesday is house, Wednesday is girls' night (free entry, free booze), Thursday is 1990s, Friday and Saturday is house again, with the occasional name – Paul Van Dyke, John Digweed – popping in. Immense in size, the club covers three levels, all with accompanying bars, and there's a cordoned-off VIP section where tables can't be seen for champagne bottles (bouncer guarded).

Le Redlight, 34 rue du Départ, St Germain
Tel: 01 42 79 94 53   www.leredlight.fr
Open: midnight–6am (noon Fri–Sat). Closed Mondays to Wednesdays.

You can't get much deeper into the concrete jungle in Paris than Le Redlight, buried in the basement of the Tour Montparnasse. There are two large dance-floors, the best laser show in town and a massive sound system

pumping out the latest tech-house, sometimes played by famous international-al DJs flown in from the UK or Ibiza, or indeed by the electro-tastic owner-David Guetta. There can be long queues, but they tend to move quickly, and the bouncers impose their own brand of face control so try to look like you mean business. The crowd is young, rich and very up for it, and on some nights the club is mixed with a gay slant. They put on well-attended after-parties from 6am on Saturday and Sunday mornings.

Rex, 5 boulevard Poissonnière, Grands Boulevards
Tel: 01 42 36 10 96   www.rexclub.com
Open: 11pm–6am daily

Rex started hosting dance-music nights way back in 1988 and is something

of an institution on the Paris club scene. Laurent Garnier has been a strong supporter from the start, and the club continues to attract some of the biggest international DJs (Daft Punk, Carl Cox, Grooverider, etc.). Techno is the main focus but the excellent sound system pumps out anything from hip-hop to drum'n'bass depending on the night. At only 400 sq m the club is not small by Parisian standards and the décor is beginning to look a little faded at the edges, but both entry and drinks are fairly reasonable. Check in advance what's on, as some of the nights are a little dead and you may be surrounded by a crowd who are more after-work than after-party. But if you do catch a good night here, it's one of the best places in the city.

La Scène Bastille, 2 bis rue des Taillandiers, Bastille
Tel: 01 48 06 50 70   www.scenebastille.com
Open: 7.30pm till 11pm for concerts, midnight–6am for clubbing

This centrally located club and concert venue describes itself as eclectic, and rightly so if you consider that both The Cure and Hanson have played gigs here. It's open every night, but it only really gets going at weekends when the live acts are followed by hugely popular club nights. As the music

varies so widely, check the website in advance (although a definite techno-house slant usually prevails). Inside, the large and moody dance-floor and bar typically get packed and hectic, but a chill-out room is available where you can get away from it all. Unusually for a Parisian club, the management doesn't seem to crave the presence of foreigners, and the bouncers may test you as to what night is on when you arrive. If you don't know this key piece of information they might not let you in, so it's best to get clued up in advance. The club hosts gay-friendly after-parties from 6am at weekends.

Le Triptyque, 142 rue Montmartre, Grands Boulevards
Tel: 01 40 28 05 55 www.letriptyque.com
Open: 9pm–1am Tues–Wed; 11pm–6am Thurs–Sat

Le Triptyque was a breath of fresh air on the Parisian club scene when it first opened in 2003, and is still one of the hippest places to party. The owners take their music very seriously and have started up their own recording studio. Nights here are usually of the highest quality, with big-name DJs

hosting *soirées* of anything from techno or house to hip-hop or drum'n'bass. Red velvet stools, armchairs and sofas have been positioned along the wide concrete corridor, right up to the large corner bar, where clubbers can chill out pre- and post-dance. Hidden around the corner is the rectangular, stone-walled dance-floor, at the end of which is a high-rise stage, complete with DJ booth. Because of the inviting bar space, people do tend to come in early to avoid the queue, which goes against typical Parisian clubbing etiquette.

Le Troisième Lieu, 62 rue Quincampoix, Beaubourg
Tel: 01 48 04 85 64 www.letroisiemelieu.com
Open: 6pm–2am (6am Fri–Sat) daily

Straight folk are welcome in this super-funky lesbian haunt, where a good mix of girls come to drink, snack and dance the night away. You can sit up at the long bar (where you can admire the collection of G-strings dangling above the beer pumps), chat away at the several rows of benches and colourful Formica tables, or settle down in the back room, which is decorated in ironic granny wallpaper and chandeliers. Table football is a popular aside to the flirting, with tournaments held every Wednesday from 6pm.

Proper football matches are projected on screens, transforming into twisted club visuals later in the evening. Serious DJs come to play Wednesday through to Saturday nights, livening up the crowd, who eventually migrate to the clubbier basement area and move on to more unruly behaviour.

Vinyl Paris, 25 boulevard Poissonnière, Grands Boulevards
Tel: 01 40 26 28 30 www.vinyl-paris.com
Open: midnight–dawn Tues–Sat

In a basement next to the funkier girls' club Le Pulp, this is one for the boys (although there is a mixed crowd most nights). The music policy concentrates on house but occasionally lapses into disco and French pop. On

nights hosted by well-known DJs the atmosphere can be electric, but check in advance since the place can be a little soulless and exhibit a rather confused identity, with bad boys wearing baseball caps mixing with Dior-clad posers. The industrial-design interior looks as if it could have been stolen from the futuristic section of The Crystal Maze. The intimate VIP balcony above the DJ booth is much sought after, and is a good place to observe the shenanigans below. Girls get in for free on Monday and Wednesday night, and there are occasional themed student nights – a change from the usual glam-chic motif.

Wagg, 62 rue Mazarine, St Germain
Tel: 01 55 42 22 01   www.wagg.fr
Open: 11.30pm–6am Fri–Sat; 3pm–midnight Sun

Previously Whisky A Go-Go, Jim Morrison's famous hangout, where he is said to have spent his last night. One of the doors in the long corridor –

before you reach the main room – has been left unchanged since those days, since its psychedelic patterns were thought to have been painted by Morrison himself (although it is unsigned). A dance-floor is surrounded by booths with tables and couches, and a long bar. Every Friday, WAGG is home to a British import, 1970s funk night Carwash (the establishment belongs to Terence Conran), so expect flairs and afro wigs. Saturday is host to various club nights, the most popular being a 1980s extravaganza, along with your usual generic house genre. Sunday is salsa, with lessons from 3pm for those that need it. A night called 'I Love Club St Germain' usually features on Thursdays during June and July, but it is best to call them up or check the website first (www.clubstgermain.com).

LIVE MUSIC

L'Attirail, 9 rue au Maire, Marais
Tel: 01 42 72 44 42 www.lattirail.com
Open: 6pm–2am daily

Half the walls at L'Attirail are like old billboards – they're coated in layer upon layer of posters, half torn and peeling, revealing the misshapen past underneath and creating an unplanned collage of colour. The other half is like a missing persons gallery: row upon row of inexplicable mug shots. Are

they regulars? Are they missing? Algerian-born Ali and his brother, who run the joint, couldn't (or wouldn't) tell, but that's probably because they're simply too laid-back to bother. A young, trendy crowd comes here at all times of day to down cold beers or feast on Ali's home-made couscous. Daily concerts are from 8.30pm (that is, if the said band bother turning up) and range from gypsy folk music to staple jazz. If the musicians do end up going missing (look out for their mug shots on the wall) it's no great loss, as Ali has an abundance of interesting CDs to play and the happening crowd will create an atmosphere of their own.

Le Cameleon, 57 rue Saint-André-des-Arts, St Germain
Tel: 01 44 41 19 49
Open: 6pm–2am daily. Concerts start at 9pm.

You will know when a band is playing in the vaulted room downstairs at Le Cameleon because there will be a crowd waiting to squeeze in at the door. And squeeze in they will – to the point where you'll be hardly able to

breathe (although holding your breath is probably a good idea, since the space reeks of stale sweat and cigarette smoke). But this is a good thing: jazz clubs are meant to be cramped, dark, dingy and damp. Use your luminous cocktail cherry to light the way down deeper into the vault and you'll never want to come out to see the light of day. It's also got a slightly more sophisticated sister jazz club around the corner, Le Tennessee Bar (12 rue André Mazet), where you can expect a cool crowd listening to Frank on low, black chesterfield sofas.

Franc Pinot de L'Île Saint Louis, I quai de Bourbon, Île Saint Louis
Tel: 01 46 33 60 64 www.franc-pinot.com
Concerts start at 9pm Mon–Thurs, 10pm Fri–Sat, 8pm Sun. Closed Mondays and throughout August (as well as some Sundays, so it's best to check).

The famous photographer Atget photographed the doorway to Franc Pinot when it was still a bistro – that's how old it is. The blue façade, with wrought grapevine insignia and grille, remains unchanged, only now it's one of the most atmospheric jazz joints in Paris. (Good jazz clubs usually have a blue-and-white 'TSF 89.9 fm' sign in the window.) Upstairs, lit up by a sparkly neon 'Jazz' sign, is the booth-style bar, where photographs of jazz giants line the walls. The serious business happens downstairs in the vaulted cellar, where you sit at small tables, lit by tiny red lamps. There is also a mezzanine level from which you can spot the occasional celebrity musician in the audience. The bar is open from 7pm and concerts start from 9pm; prices

vary from €10 to €15, depending on the artist. Take note that, regardless of the quality of the music, it's impossible to predict whether the club will be full or empty.

ADULT ENTERTAINMENT

Paris' illicit venues are called 'clubs' – a normal nightclub will be referred to as a *boîte (de nuit)*. Prostitution is illegal in Paris, although there is a kerb-crawling scene (rue Saint-Denis in the 1st arrondissement and rue Joubert in the 9th), and the area of Pigalle is notorious for its sleazy sex trade. You'll find plenty of brothel bars, which are tolerated by the police, and the ones on the streets leading away from Place Pigalle are a little snazzier and rather atmospheric – you will often find an aged ruby-lipsticked madame fanning herself at the entrance, guarding her girls like a mother hen. If such an indicative presence cannot be found, look out for the hugely overpriced drinks menu pasted outside, and you'll know what kind of establishment it is.

FETISH CLUBS

Cris et Chuchautements, 9 rue Truffaut, Montmartre
Tel: 01 42 93 70 21 www.cris-et-chuchotements.com

The name translates as 'Screams and Whispers'... so what else could it be but an S&M/fetish club, complete with torture rack and doctor's chair?

STRIP CLUBS

Pink Paradise, 49–51 rue de Ponthieu, Champs-Élysées
Tel: 01 58 36 19 20 www.pinkparadise.fr

Designer strip club around the corner from the Champs-Élysées.

Stringfellow's, 27 avenue des Ternes, Champs-Élysées
Tel: 01 47 66 45 00 www.stringfellows-paris.net

Peter and his Cabaret of Angels come to Paris.

SWINGERS' CLUBS

Les Chandelles, 1 rue Thérèse, Louvre
Tel: 01 42 60 43 31 www.les-chandelles.com

Paris' high-end exclusive swingers' club (*club échangiste*) – it's worth checking out the website to see just how swanky it is. Singles welcome on Mondays.

L'Overside, 92 rue du Cherche-midi, Galerie Le Sevrien
Tel: 01 42 84 10 20 www.overside.fr

Club reserved for couples during the week, starting from 10.30pm. Single men accepted Sunday and Wednesday. Bar, shows, dance-floor, party rooms, showers, six themed shows.

Notes & Updates

culture...

With over 1,800 classified monuments, 170 museums, 145 theatres and 380 cinemas, it's impossible to summarize what goes on in Paris culturally. Parisians take culture very seriously, and with an unashamedly high dose of intellectual snobbishness. Given that the Lumière brothers invented cinema, that the Louvre houses the world's largest art collection, and that famous Parisians include Jean-Paul Sartre and Edith Piaf, this snobbishness is hard to counter.

Mayor Bertrand Delanoë has brilliantly capitalized on it by creating the yearly 'Nuit Blanche' in early October, when a gamut of cultural institutions – from museums and libraries to swimming pools and churches – are open all through the night, enabling you to breathe in art at the Centre Pompidou at 3am on your way to a concert, after you've immersed yourself in a little Proust or Balzac.

An ideal place for a whistle-stop tour of Parisian cultural heritage are the two cemeteries – Père-Lachaise and Montparnasse – where so many cultural icons continue to draw crowds and inspire from their resting-places, from writers such as Colette to musicians such as Bizet and Serge Gainsbourg.

Paris is a city of and for film buffs. Its unique independent cinema scene upholds old classics, documentaries and low-budget experiments that are a galaxy away from the large chain multiplexes. Many of these art houses, which projected Godard, Truffaut, Deneuve and Bardot into stardom, are found in the Latin Quarter on Rue des Écoles. Among these, Action Écoles, Champo and Grande Action are three that specialize in American classics and cult flicks. Many are steeped in history or are unique spaces worth visiting in their own right. Examples are Studio 28, which featured in the film *Amélie* and was patronized (and had its light fittings designed) by Jean Cocteau; La Pagode, an actual pagoda built in 1896 by the owner of the Bon Marché as a gift to his wife; and Le Grand Rex, an impressive Art Deco building that bears witness to the days when a trip to the cinema was saved for special occasions.

Impressionism, Cubism, Fauvism, Symbolism, Dadaism (sounds like the lyrics to a Kraftwerk song)… pretty much every significant art movement of the last hundred-odd years started here. Any fan of the Impressionists must visit the Musée d'Orsay, although the Musée Marmottan-Monet in the 16th houses the world's largest collection of Claude Monet's paintings (his famous *Water lilies*, however, are at the Musée de l'Orangerie in the Tuileries gardens). The range of galleries encompasses the newly opened and restored Grand and Petit Palais, the smaller and rather easier to digest musées Picasso and Rodin, and quirkier museums such as Musée Gustave-Moreau.

Prominent galleries showcasing contemporary art include the Palais de Tokyo, the Centre Pompidou and Jeu de Paume. Photography is well represented in venues such as the Maison Européene de la Photographie and Foundation Henri Cartier-Bresson on the impasse Lebouis. Primitive and tribal art can be mulled over at the new Musée du Quai Branly beside the Eiffel Tower.

If you prefer the performing arts, then there's the Moulin Rouge (Pigalle) or the Lido (Champs-Élysées) for the tacky charm of bare-breasted, leggy can-can dancers; world-class opera and ballet at the Opéra Garnier and Opéra de la Bastille (the former is the home of the Phantom); or Molière at the Comédie Française, the oldest continuing theatre company in the western world.

Classical music enthusiasts should head to the recently renovated Salle Pleyel, home to the Orchestre de Paris (www.pleyel.com). Paris' jazz scene is both vibrant and historic – Josephine Baker stormed the city in the 1920s, as Miles Davis did in the 1950s. Stadium acts perform at the Olympia, favoured by Edith back in the day, or Zénith at Parc de la Villette, and smaller pop or indie bands play at venues such as La Bataclan and Élysée Montmartre. It's worth visiting Paris for its Fête de la Musique festival on 21 June, when there are free concerts all over the city, and an array of musicians ranging from DJs to teenage rock bands take over the streets.

For a comprehensive listing of all cultural goings-on, in English, visit www.paris-info.com.

Cimetière du Montparnasse, 3 boulevard Edgar-Quinet/rue Froidevaux, Montparnasse

Tel; 01 44 10 86 50

Open: 8am (8.30am Sat, 9am Sun)–6pm (5pm mid-Nov–mid-Mar) daily

There's nothing more enjoyable than strolling through the peaceful Cimetière du Montparnasse on a sunny day or lazy Sunday. A slightly less Gothic or oppressive cemetery than the famous Père-Lachaise, Montparnasse lacks the army of tourists traipsing up and down in search of

the infamous Jim Morrison tomb. It is home, however, to France's rock star equivalent, Serge Gainsbourg (of 'Je t'aime, moi non plus' fame), whose grave has been littered with love notes, Gitane cigarettes and various bottles of booze (unlike the now sanitized and guarded Morrison tomb). You should be able to spot the occasional angst-ridden teenager slumped over Sartre's grave. Samuel Beckett, Baudelaire, de Beauvoir, Maupassant and Man Ray also rest here.

Cimetière du Père-Lachaise, boulevard de Ménilmontant, Belleville

Tel: 01 55 25 82 10   www.pere-lachaise.com

Open: daily, 8am (8.30am Sat, 9am Sun)–6pm (5pm mid-Nov–mid-Mar)

Père-Lachaise is really two different cemeteries rolled into one. Part of it feels like the set of a dark and Gothic Tim Burton movie, with grey, dilapi-dated tombs protected by vicious-looking gargoyles and steep cobblestoned winding paths. The other part is almost flat, with wide tree-lined avenues and benches where you can rest and get your bearings. Pick up a map from the main entrance (weekdays only) or buy one from florists' shops in the area, because you are going to get very lost trying to find your buried hero.

Otherwise, a crowd clustered around a grave is a tell-tale sign… or you can practise your orientation skills with the amazing virtual website. Oscar Wilde, Edith Piaf, Colette and Delacroix are among the many Greats buried here. Oh, and Jim Morrison, too.

Eiffel Tower, Champs de Mars, Invalides
Tel: 01 44 54 19 30   www.tour-eiffel.fr
Open: 9.30am–11pm (9am–midnight 16 June–2 September) daily

Built as a temporary – and at the time not universally liked – structure for the 1889 International Exhibition, the Eiffel Tower has become the iconic landmark of the French capital. Standing 324 metres high, the puddle-iron structure remained the world's tallest building until 1930 and is still one of the best spots for panoramic views of Paris. Divided into three accessible platforms, the first and second levels can be reached either using the stairs or one of three lifts, while the third is connected by lift from the second floor. There are several queues to conquer: one to buy your ticket (no advance internet sales), one to reach the first or second floor, and (the longest and certainly the most painful) one for the top. It's best to decide at the bottom of the tower just how much queueing you're prepared to put up with, as a top-floor ticket is the most expensive (but you'll be rewarded with a reconstruction of Gustave Eiffel's office, complete with his waxwork, at the top). In addition to the view, there are historical panels, a 'Cineiffel' and Post Office (to stamp your Eiffel postcard with its own postmark), self-

service restaurant and souvenir shop. The second level also has Michelin-starred restaurant Le Jules Verne (booking essential; call 01 45 55 61 44).

Le Jardin du Luxembourg, St Germain-des-Près
Tel: 01 42 34 23 89   www.paris.fr
Open: daily, 7.30am–9.45pm summer; 8.15am–4.45pm winter

Stretching out over an area of 60 acres, Le Jardin du Luxembourg is the largest park within the city's limits. Opened to the public in the 19th century, the park and palace were built in 1612 for the Medici family. The palace, modelled on the Pitti Palace in Florence, sits at the northern end of the park and has enjoyed a colourful history, having served as a prison during the French Revolution, the Luftwaffe headquarters during World War II, and most recently as the seat of the French Senate. The baroque gardens are beautifully laid out with statues and fountains breaking up the regimented

lawns and borders. The lawns are strewn with cast-iron benches, as it's forbidden to sit on the grass (and the park policemen enjoy hiding in the bushes to catch transgressors). For children there are pony rides, a boating pond and a puppet theatre. The western area of the park is given over to sport while in the north-west corner chess enthusiasts congregate to pit their wits against all-comers. In the summer open-air concerts and operas are staged.

Le Jeu de Paume, I place de la Concorde, Louvre

Tel: 01 47 03 12 50 www.jeudepaume.org
Open: noon (10am Sat–Sun)–7pm (9pm Tues). Closed Mondays, New Year's Day, I May and Christmas Day.

If you are into photography, cinema and video art, the Jeu de Paume Museum is well worth adding to your itinerary. However, bear in mind that in this case, one name means two locations. The charming Site Concorde is in the Tuileries, where it played a crucial role in the French Revolution as the seat of government until a representative constitution was in place (M Guillotine is credited with selecting the building) and was once home to the Impressionist paintings now located at the Museé d'Orsay. Its doppelganger, known as the Site Sully, is housed in a 17th-century building in the increasingly trendy Bastille area (62 rue Saint-Antoine, tel: 01 42 74 47 75). The Jeu de Paume Museum functions as a gallery hosting several exhibitions a year, showing the work of past and contemporary artists from all over the world. Some shows travel over from museums

such as MoMA in New York, while others are less international. Free guided tours are available and there is a programme of talks and film seasons, but only the Site Concorde has a café.

Louvre, Cours Napoleon, Louvre

Tel: 01 40 20 57 60 www.louvre.fr

Open: 9am–6pm (9.45pm Wed–Fri). Closed Tuesdays, New Year's Day, 1 May, 25 August and Christmas Day.

Where do you begin with the Louvre? Set in Louis XIV's palace, with the magnificent Tuileries as its back garden, and housing around 35,000 works of art, this wonderful museum demands a planned visit – so decide in advance what you would like to see, buy your entrance tickets online and avoid queuing. The main entrance to the museum is through I.M. Pei's famous glass-and-steel pyramid in the Cour Napoleon. Once inside, the huge collection includes European art from the Middle Ages to the mid-19th century, artefacts from the Islamic world, Egypt and Rome, and examples of decorative art. Among the best known pieces are, of course, the world's most famous painting, *The Mona Lisa* (on the first floor of the Denon wing),

known as *La Joconde* in French, Gericault's apocalyptic *Radeau de la Meduse* and *Liberty Leading the People* by Delacroix. If time allows, don't miss the Michelangelo Gallery of Italian sculpture. In addition to the permanent collections, the Louvre organizes regular exhibitions, art classes and workshops. Numerous cultural events take place in the 450-seat auditorium located just beneath I.M. Pei's pyramid. When all the culture starts wearing you down, you can repair to the restaurant or one of five cafés, or just browse in the well-stocked bookshop.

Maison Européene de la Photographie, 5–7 rue de Fourcy, Marais

Tel: 01 44 78 75 00   www.mep-fr.org
Open: 11am–8pm. Closed Mondays and Tuesdays.

Housed in a renovated and extended 17th-century mansion, the Maison Européene de la Photographie aims to give the public the best possible access to film media in its three most prevalent forms: photographic prints, the printed page and video. The museum is spread over three floors and comprises an exhibition centre, library and auditorium, as well as a book-shop and a café.

Concentrating on contemporary photographic art from the 1950s to the present day, the museum embraces all styles from reportage to fashion photography, with an incredible compilation of more than 15,000 works. Major European artists form the core of the collection, but there's a strong Japanese connection also. As well as its permanent displays, the museum hosts temporary exhibitions, devoted in equal measure to photographers' retrospectives and up-and-coming talent. The space is rarely crowded and the exhibitions always fascinating, making this a perfect place to escape from the hustle and bustle of the Marais.

La Maison Rouge – Fondation Antoine de Galbert, 10 boulevard de la Bastille, Bastille

Tel: 01 40 01 08 81   www.lamaisonrouge.org
Open: 11am–7pm (9pm Thurs). Closed Mondays and Tuesdays.

An art foundation created in 2004 by the private collector Antoine de Galbert, a prominent figure on the French contemporary art scene.

Exhibitions from his collection and temporary exhibitions of contemporary art are featured here, with the aim of promoting art to a wider audience. The foundation also commissions artists independently, helping them to express themselves without financial constraint, in the hope it will lead to exciting new work. The old factory warehouse space is enormous, with four large rooms dedicated to showcasing modern art, all built within the red building from which the foundation gets its name. There's a cool café inside, as well as 'Bookstorming', a specialist art bookshop.

Mémorial des Martyrs de La Déportation, Square de L'Île de France, Île de la Cité
Tel: 01 46 33 87 56
Open: 10am–noon, 2–7pm (5pm Nov–Feb) daily

At the eastern tip of the Île de la Cité, down a couple of steps, is a well-

hidden memorial dedicated to the memory of those deported from France to German concentration camps during World War II. Appropriately situated in what was once a morgue, simple chambers are lined with 200,000 lights representing the 200,000 individuals that died at the hands of the Nazis. The 1960s design manages to be both beautiful and thought-provokingly bleak. The black spiky sculpture and barred window, which looks out to the Seine, gives a feeling of imprisonment and claustrophobia. The poetry engraved on the walls of the chambers invites a moment of peaceful and spiritual reflection.

Musée National Gustave-Moreau, 14, rue de La Rochefoucauld, Montmartre
Tel: 01 48 74 38 50 www.musee-moreau.fr
Open: 10am–12.45pm, 2pm–5.15pm. Closed Tuesdays.

A wonderful museum that feels like somebody's 19th-century private home. Well, it was Gustave Moreau's private home before he turned it into a showcase for his artworks two years before he died, giving it to the state on the condition it was left untouched – a fantastically vainglorious approach to preserving his legacy. Almost every inch of the great 'salle' is

covered in paintings, the popular way of displaying art at the time. A couple of chests-of-drawers and a row of flip-rails hidden behind white curtains contain the preparatory sketches for you to browse through. A beautiful wrought-iron spiral staircase leads you up to his living quarters, the décor of which puts modern-day designer Jacques Garcia, of Hôtel Costes fame, to shame.

Musée National Picasso, Hôtel Salé, 5 rue de Thorigny, Marais

Tel: 01 42 71 25 21 www.musee-picasso.fr

Open: 9.30am–6pm (5.30pm Oct–Mar). Closed Tuesdays, New Year's Day and Christmas Day.

Set in the fashionable Marais district in the heart of Paris, the Picasso museum is housed in a magnificent 17th-century hotel and contains the world's most complete Picasso archive. Arranged chronologically, the collection encompasses Picasso's entire artistic evolution, including his early days in Barcelona, Cubism, sculpture, his sources of inspiration and his own art collection. The core of the holdings was formed when Picasso's heirs made a huge donation to the French state, gifting hundreds of paintings, drawings and sculptures in lieu of duty after Picasso's death in 1973. In 1978, the French state augmented the museum's holdings when it received a gift of Picasso's personal art

collection, including works by Matisse, Cézanne and other major artists. Further donations of personal archives, and a gift in lieu of death duties from Picasso's wife, Jacqueline, rounded off the collection. A cafeteria in the small garden serves light refreshments during the summer months (15 April–15 October).

Museé d'Orsay, 62 rue de Lille, Invalides

Tel: 01 40 49 48 14 (guided tours) www.musee-orsay.fr

Open: 9.30am–6pm (9.45pm Thurs). Closed Mondays, New Year's Day, 1 May and Christmas Day.

Anyone interested in Impressionist and Post-Impressionist art should make

sure this museum is on his or her visit list. Located in a beautifully refurbished turn-of-the century train station on the left bank of the Seine, the
Museé d'Orsay holds an extensive collection of western (mostly French) art
from 1848 to the start of World War 1. This not only includes paintings, but
also sculptures, architecture, photography and the decorative arts – with an
impressive range of Art Nouveau pieces. Among the works on display, the
visitor will find Edouard Manet's groundbreaking and much talked-about *Le
Déjeuner sur l'Herbe*, Edgar Degas' *L'Absinthe*, as well as paintings by Monet,

Renoir, Whistler and Van Gogh. And when you need to rest from this creative kaleidoscope, head for one of the two cafés (Le Café des Hauteurs on
the fifth floor, and the Mezzanine Café above it) for refreshments. A restaurant with a 19th-century interior opens for lunch and tea, and dinner on
Thursdays (tel: 01 45 49 47 03 for more information).

Musée Rodin, 79 rue de Varenne, Invalides

Tel: 01 44 18 61 10 www.musee-rodin.fr
Open: daily, 9.30am–5.45pm (garden 6.45pm) Apr–Sept; 9.30am–4.45pm
(garden 5pm) Oct–Mar

A stone's throw from Les Invalides and an essential stop for any visitor to
Paris, Musée Rodin feels like a visit to the artist's recently vacated home.
Carved panelling, a glass gallery and an extensive garden restored in 1993
serve as backdrop to Rodin's marble and bronze sculptures, archives and
personal collection, which include Roman statues displayed against the back-
ground of trees and greenery. Much of the collection was created as the
result of a 1916 donation from the artist to the French state with the

proviso that the museum should be housed in the beguiling, ramshackle 18th-century mansion in which Rodin had already installed some of his works. All the artist's major works are represented, some as later acquisitions, including the famous *Thinker* and *The Kiss*. The museum also plays host to temporary exhibitions throughout the year.

Palais de Tokyo, 13 avenue de Président-Wilson, Trocadero
Tel: 01 47 23 38 86 www.palaisdetokyo.com
Open: noon–midnight. Closed Mondays, New Year's Day, 1 May and Christmas Day.

Don't be confused by the name, this isn't a museum dedicated to Japan, but a showcase for contemporary art. Built for the International Exposition of Arts and Techniques of 1937 (people just got into the habit of calling the building the Palais de Tokyo, because the riverbank below was known as the

quai de Tokyo), it housed Paris' National Museum of Modern Art before it moved to the Georges Pompidou Center. French architects Anne Lacaton and Jean-Philippe Vassal are responsible for its latest incarnation as a centre for contemporary art, which opened in 2002. Curators Nicolas Bourriaud and Jérôme Sans put together an interesting blend of cross-disciplinary media in a fittingly bare 'warehouse' space to give the art maximum impact. The Palais de Tokyo also has four cinema screens dedicated to experimental and art-house film. The extraordinary opening hours, along with its trendy restaurant, shops and café, pull in a cool, young urban crowd.

ENTERTAINMENT

Cirque d'Hiver Bouglione, 110 rue Amelot, Oberkampf
Tel: 01 47 00 12 25 / 01 47 00 28 81 www.cirquedhiver.com
Performances: Oct–late Feb

What, no tent? Cirque d'Hiver is one of the few remaining permanent (and stationary) circuses today and is apparently where Jules Léotard invented the trapeze, and subsequently, to make the act both safer and more pleasing to the eye, the famous garment that bears his name. What's more, the polygonal building looks like something out of *Asterix and Obelix*, and has been run by the same Bouglione family since it opened in 1852. Traditional circus performances with the likes of trapeze artists, contortionists and animal acts, as well as the usual motley crew of clowns, take place during the winter months. To make an evening of it, go to the clown-themed restaurant down the road that serves delicious home-made French traditional cooking, with fabulous wine, ideal for a pre- or post-circus dinner (Le Clown Bar: 114 rue Amelot, tel: 01 43 55 87 35).

Opéra de la Bastille, Place de la Bastille, Bastille
Tel: 01 44 73 13 99 www.operadeparis.fr

Home of the Opéra National de Paris, this glass and metal building has been variously described as anything from an inspired piece of modern architecture to a hippopotamus in a bathtub. However, regardless of what you think of the exterior, the huge space allows for some of the most lavish and

207

grandiose productions in the world, using enormous sets and the latest technology to impressive effect. The construction of this opera house was one of President Mitterrand's Grands Projets, whose aim was to make opera more accessible to the public. The 2,723-seat theatre opened in 1989 on the 200th anniversary of the storming of the Bastille prison, and has put on a varied programme of opera and ballet ever since. Performances can be booked up months in advance so organize your visit ahead of time (although a limited number of standing tickets are available each evening).

Opéra Garnier, Place de l'Opéra, Opéra
Tel: 01 40 01 25 14 www.operadeparis.fr

Fictional home of Gaston Leroux's *Phantom of the Opera*, this magnificent neo-baroque edifice houses the Paris Opera Ballet. Designed by Charles Garnier in the mid-19th century, and described by a contemporary as an 'overcrowded sideboard', it has come to be recognized as a masterpiece of its style. The exterior drips with statuary and friezes while the interior is a riot of gold leaf, red velvet and crystal. The auditorium contains 1,979 seats and has a beautiful ceiling painted by Marc Chagall in 1964, above the enormous six-ton chandelier. Home to top dance productions, the facilities allow the most extravagant performances to be staged – the revolving stage can even accommodate a group of running horses. And just as in the story of the Phantom, the basement contains an underground lake. Guided tours of the building are on offer during the day for €6, but you should check in advance if the company is rehearsing on stage (you won't be allowed into the auditorium). If you are lucky enough to get a ticket to a performance, dress up and do it in style.

Music at Châtelet
Daily (although less on Sundays); free with metro ticket

Pass through Châtelet métro during the day, and you'll come across some excellent (and perhaps a few not so excellent) musicians busking in its many underground tunnels and passageways. At one of the main exits there's enough space to hold a 10-piece band and spectators stop and watch, clogging up the stairway and forcing others to trip past them. It's a good idea to keep a few *pièces* (coins) handy, as there are buskers throughout the Paris métro, some of whom will perform on the train, hopping from carriage to carriage (so there's no escape). There's a wide variety of quality and versatility, ranging from a saxophone rendition of 'Ace of Base' to juvenile hip-hop (cover your ears) and performance art.

Le Grand Rex, 1 boulevard Poissonnière, Grands Boulevards
www.legrandrex.com

This enormous cinema wasn't called Le 'Grand' Rex for nothing, and over 60 years on, it is still Paris's largest movie theatre. A plush baroque-style interior and magnificent Art Deco exterior makes this an original and a must for cinema enthusiasts who appreciate the old-school grandeur. Sitting on the high-level red velvet seats while crunching on buttered popcorn is such a worthwhile experience it doesn't really matter if the film is in a language you don't understand. If you're lucky, you'll be able to catch an Anglophone film shown with French subtitles (look out for the 'VO' symbol standing for Version Original), but if not, and you'd rather not watch a French flick you don't understand, or if you're allergic to the notion of 'dubbing', you can opt for a guided tour around the building, skipping the movie part all together.

Studio 28, 10 rue Tholozé, Montmartre
Tel: 01 46 06 36 07   www.cinemastudio28.com

Montmartre's arty crowd watch art-house and classic films at this retro cinema, which remains much unchanged since it first opened in the 1920s (except, thanks to government funding, it now has an up-to-date screen with Dolby surround sound). It was the meeting-place for many avant-garde film-makers, most notably Luis Buñuel and Abel Gance, and was patronized by Jean Cocteau (who even designed the light-fittings). You can enjoy a cocktail at the tiny foyer bar or sit in the covered courtyard café, although it gets very busy at the weekends. A scene from the movie *Amelie* was shot here.

shop...

Parisians are some of the best-dressed people in the world, so it's easy to feel scruffy in Paris. They will shamelessly eye you up and down – and that includes the snooty sales staff as you walk in a shop. So it's best to smarten up if you want to avoid feeling fashionably worthless. The Parisian look is one of conformist elegance. Choose an eccentric outfit and you'll be met with open-mouthed stares, while anything too grungy or sporty will provoke an obvious wince. There is no shopping 'centre' in Paris as such: instead, every *quartier* offers its own unique shopping experience.

The Champs-Élysées is Paris' equivalent to Oxford Street, dominated by chain stores such as Zara and Gap, and good for late-night retail therapy, although its wide, café-filled pavements and view of the Arc de Triomphe mark it out as one of the most famous shopping streets in the world.

The 'golden triangle' in the 8th arrondissement, as well as the rue du Faubourg-Saint-Honoré and its environs, are where all the most exclusive shops are located, representing the *prêt-à-porter* collections of haute-couture designers. The greatest danger here, beyond bankruptcy, is having your legs clipped by the enormous shopping bags of ladies-who-shop, their expensive perfume preceding them as they approach, who get annoyed if you so much as nudge their microscopic Chihuahuas with your foot.

The Left Bank, around Saint-Germain-des-Prés, is full of winding boutique-lined streets, where antique shops, small galleries and book handlers trade alongside elegant brands as well as quirkier designers such as Martin Margiela. Some boutiques, like Margiela's, are worth visiting purely for their conceptual store design. Examples are Comme des Garçons' 'red' store on rue du Faubourg-Saint-Honoré (no. 54), and Balenciaga on avenue George V.

The latest craze is the multi-brand concept store. Make sure you check out L'Eclaireur and Shine in the Marais, and Colette and Maria Luisa around rue

Saint-Honoré. Colette is the most famous, being the first. It's more of a fashion exhibition than a shop, but worth a look if you want to find out what everybody will be wearing this season. For less expensive, hip, original fashion and street wear, head to the Marais, or seek out the ateliers of young designers in Abbesses or near Saint-Martin canal.

The department stores, or *grands magasins*, are Le Bon Marché, Printemps and Galeries Lafayette. Le Bon Marché is the most glamorous (it's in the 6th). All have a good mix of trendy designers as well as 'old-school' French couturiéres such as Lanvin, YSL and Chanel. They tend to be very good for 'indoor window-shopping', because the sales staff don't approach you directly – in fact, you are lucky if you can find someone to help! The jeans section in Printemps is particularly worthy of note as it always seems to stock the latest 'must have' brands.

Paris also has an array of beautiful old-style glass-roofed arcades, some of which are a little run-down, although Galerie Vivienne (2nd) is a must and Passage Jouffroy (9th), with its specialist antique shops, feels like a museum.

If you are looking for a particular brand but don't fancy venturing into the *grands magasins*, the chances are that you will find its boutique on the glamorous avenue Montaigne: Chanel, Chloé, MaxMara – you name it, it's there. If you can, have lunch at L'Avenue where even old men sport fake tans.

Shops are usually open between 10am and 7pm Monday to Saturday – although bear in mind that some of the smaller shops may close for lunch, take an extra day off during the week (usually a Monday or Tuesday) and certainly close up for August. *Les grands magasins* stay open until 9pm on Thursdays and often some of the smaller shops follow suit. Take note when planning a shopping trip to Paris that the sales have a statutory beginning and end date, so unless you are invited to pick the best pieces at pre-sale events, all shops will start their sale on the same day. This means that the first day tends to be hectic (there will be queues outside Le Bon Marché waiting for it to open), but the bargains make up for it. Don't go at the end of the sales period when all the gems have been snapped up and the new seasonal collection doesn't match the weather outside.

AVENUE MONTAIGNE

Avenue Montaigne is the 24-carat section of the golden triangle. This is where you'll find the highest proportion of chic Parisiennes taking a window-shopping stroll with their equally immaculate, coiffured poodles. Many of the haute couture houses have their main offices here. You can eat while enjoying a magnificent view of the city at the restaurant Maison Blanche (see Eat) or sit alongside moneyed gentlemen sporting greased-back hair and their model girlfriends at the Costes-owned L'Avenue (no. 41). Stopping off at the Plaza Athénée – for breakfast or tea in its Galerie des Gobelins (see Snack), indulging in a lunch prepared by Alain Ducasse or simply for post-shopping cocktails – is an absolute must.

Prada (10) Prada's famous handbags, shoes and prêt-à-porter clothes collection

Joseph (14) Signature tuxedo trousers for women, great knitwear, understated sexiness

Valentino (19) Couture house renowned for quietly glamorous evening-wear, with a dedicated international clientele

Dolce & Gabbana (22) The boys bring you OTT glamour, with Madonna as their muse

Christian Dior (30) John Galliano gives a sexy and dynamic oomph to the couture label's image

MaxMara (31) Women's wear, from casual chic to downright elegant: day and evening wear

Chanel (42) Together with YSL, the brand synonymous with Parisian glamour and elegance

Bulgari (45) Jewellery to flaunt at Cannes, from the delicate to the ostentatious

Louis Vuitton (54) The handbags have sadly become arm-candy for footballers' wives, but can one be a true hedonist without possessing one of their travelling cases, which open up as a wardrobe and never need unpacking?

Calvin Klein (55) Broad-ranging, offering suits and cocktail dresses to more sporty American-style lingerie

Marni (57) Italian label mixes leather and fur with other luxury materials. Also men's wear

Gucci (60) Ever-classic, elegant clothes, shoes and accessories from the Italian mob

FAUBOURG-SAINT-HONORÉ

Along with avenue Montaigne and avenue George-V (Balenciaga, Givenchy, Gaultier), rue du Faubourg-Saint-Honoré is the most famous shopping street for aspirational retail. All the best *prêt-à-porter* couture designers are here, including the youngest of the couture houses, Christian Lacroix, which opened here in 1987. It's busier than Montaigne, probably because tourists love its typically Parisian look (a narrow street with roaring traffic and grand 19th-century mansions) while shoppers love it because it's just sooooo long. It's an inexhaustible stretch of small boutiques (and an easy route – it's a straight line), which runs for miles from the 8th arrondissement to the 1st (where it becomes simply 'rue Sainte-Honoré').

Loft Design by (12) Clothes that manage to be both smart and trendy for men and women

La Perla (20) Italian lingerie to die for, including glamorous swimming suits

Hermès (24) Horsey-themed scarves and country chic, although quirky designer Martin Margiela, and now Jean-Paul Gaultier, have given it new flair

Roger Vivier (29) Extravagant shoes from the designer largely credited for inventing the stiletto

Comme des Garçons (54) Rei Kawakubo's avant-garde fashion sculpted for both sexes

Chloé (54–56) *Prêt-à-porter* collection from the French fashion house with Phoebe Philo at its helm, offering classics with a twist

Christian Lacroix (73) Flamboyant fashion from one of the biggest creative names

Dalloyau (101) Historic pâtisserie (1802) with sinful chocolate croissants and extravagant cakes

THE CHAMPS-ÉLYSÉES

The Champs-Élysées is Paris' main shopping drag. Sadly, this means it's no longer the Elysian Fields from which it gets its name, but an area dominated by fast-food outlets and high-street chains (such as Zara, Benetton and Morgan). Nevertheless, in typical Parisian style, there are chic elements to it (Charles Jourdan, Louis Vuitton) - it does, after all, form part of the 'golden triangle' (along with avenues George-V and Montaigne). The walk from the

213

place de la Concorde, down the Champs' dusty gravel pathway that's surrounded by greenery and tree-shaded benches (to one side are the art galleries Le Grand and Le Petit Palais – both worth visiting) is wonderful. At the intersection of avenue Montaigne and Matignon (where the really posh shops are), the greenery ends and the concrete shopping strip begins.

With a view dominated by the grandiose Arc de Triomphe, the wide pavements never feel overcrowded even when busy. Along the way are many good cafés with terraces from which you can watch the world go by, such as the elegant Ladurée (no. 75; see Snack) and the trendy restaurant-cum-bar Mood (no. 114; see Eat). For an unpretentious, tourist-free lunch, go to the Jewish-run (closed on Fridays) Deloren Café (45 avenue Friedland, www.delorencafe.com) just around the corner from the Arc de Triomphe.

The Champs-Élysées is great for late-night shopping too: the Drugstore Publicis stays open till 2am and you can browse through an endless selection of CDs and DVDs in Virgin Megastore or its French equivalent, Fnac, right up until midnight, even on a Sunday. See www.champselysees.org for a comprehensive list of shops.

LOUVRE PALAIS ROYAL

Just because the rue du Faubourg-St-Honoré loses its 'Faubourg' when it hits the 1st arrondissement, it doesn't mean it loses any of its shopping appeal. In fact, many younger, funkier shops spring up here, such as the very cool concept store Colette. The many shorter side streets are also alive with fabulous fashion, and it's worth taking a zigzag stroll down all of them. Cambon is where Coco Chanel first set up shop and is home to funky Italian label Costume National. All the luxury jewellery shops are to be found on the place Vendôme (Boucheron, Van Cleef & Arpels, Cartier, Dior and Chanel's Joaillerie), which leads to the shop-lined rue de la Paix, where one can stop off for lunch at historic Café de la Paix with views to the Opéra Garnier. The irresistibly chic woman's wear of Claudie Pierlot on rue du 29 Juillet should not be missed. The angular colonnades and garden of the Palais Royal are worth visiting, even if it's just to look at Balenciaga's vintage showroom.

RUE CAMBON

Maria Luisa (2) Fantastic collection of various avant-garde designers
Costume National (5) Yohji Yamamoto employee Ennio Capasa continues to bring out sexy collections for both men and women
Fifi Chachnil (26) Burlesque sexy, very sexy lingerie – oh oui, oui!
Chanel (29) Karl Lagerfeld designs for the haute-couture house synonymous with Paris. Coco's first boutique was at no. 21 Cambon.

RUE SAINT-HONORÉ

Colette (213) Paris' first concept store is still the most popular, stocking the trendiest brands in everything from cosmetics, CDs, design books and fashion. The Water Bar has 73 different types of water, as well as designer snacks from the likes of the Rose Bakery and Ladurée.
Spa: L'appartement 217 (217) Collapse under the smoothing hands of a masseur for the ultimate shopping rejuvenation.
John Galliano (384–6) The eccentric British designer still works for Dior while continuing with his own exciting collection.

OTHERS

Pierre Hardy, *156 galerie de Valois* Designer shoes for men and women
Salons du Palais Royal, *25 rue de Valois* probably the most decadently decorated shop in the world, with sumptuous scents from the perfume makers to match.

THE LEFT BANK – SAINT-GERMAIN-DES-PRÉS

The best shopping in the Left Bank is undeniably in the 6th arrondissement, although this crosses over into the north-eastern side of the 7th, with the wonderful rue de Grenelle and rue du Bac (look out for the Deyolle shop with its eccentric taxidermy!), which conveniently starts (or ends) with the luxury department store, Le Bon Marché. The leafy boulevard Saint-Germain is really the principal shopping street, with more upmarket shops (and a less 'high-street' vibe) than the rue de Rennes, boulevard Raspail or Saint Michel. Stopping off for a coffee or 'coupé' at the Les Deux Magots or Café Flore, next to Paris' oldest church, the St-Germain-des-Prés, is an absolute must.

BOULEVARD SAINT-GERMAIN

Diptyque (34) The most beautiful-smelling candles, made with such good ingredients they perfume a room even unlit.

Onward (147) Formerly one of the most avant-garde boutiques in Paris, it still has a comprehensive stock from the likes of Vivienne Westwood and Chloé (it's got three floors!)

Emporio Armani (149) His most affordable (albeit least interesting) line for both sexes. There's a café and bookshop too.

La Hune (170) This Left Bank institution stocks a selection of art and design books, as well as a collection of French literature and theory.

Sonia Rykiel (175) The creations of the flame-haired, original Left-Bank-chic designer are wearable, young, fun. Her stripy knitwear is a French classic. Her daughter now also runs a line of yoga/dance wear plus, oddly, sex toys. The men's wear shop is at no. 194.

Shu Uemura (176) Stunning range of cosmetics with a great breadth of colour – fabulous shades for eyes, lips and nails. The facial oil cleanser is a modern skin-care classic.

La Perla (179) Elegant and sexy Italian designer lingerie.

Fragonard (196) All things to make you smell sweet, from perfumes to soaps and natural cosmetics.

Madelaine Gely & Alexandra Sojfer (218) Beautiful umbrellas, parasols and canes – antique and new.

RUE DE GRENELLE

The greatest concentration of fashion boutiques on the rue de Grenelle runs from the tip of the 6th arrondissement to its intersection with the equally fashion-filled rue du Bac in the 7th. Although the fantastic variety of boutiques ranges from the ultra-exclusive perfumes commissioned by Frédéric Malle to the quirky fashion lines of Martin Margiela, the street seems as if it were made especially for shoe-aholics. Sophisticates might want to pick up a pair of kitten heels from Charles Jourdan or Patrick Cox, while those with more outlandish taste can indulge their feverish fetish at Christian Louboutin. Le Café Basile (see Snack) is perfectly located for a pre-shopping breakfast or quick mid-shopping snack.

Yohji Yamamoto (3) Avant-garde clothes with an oriental twist. The abstract silhouette is beautiful, dignified and interesting. Perfect for a mature woman with deep pockets and an independent mind.

Martin Margiela (13) From the former iconoclastic Belgian and seminal fashion treasure. His personal aesthetic carries through from the design of the shop to his ever-increasing lines. Real, interesting clothing that everyone in fashion owns (young and old!).

Stephane Kélian (13 bis) Designer shoes that'll make you feel a million dollars

Martine Sitbon (13 bis) French cult designer twisted classics. Does for Parisian girls what Paul Smith does for English gents. Young, safe and pretty, but not boring. Good for party shoes, cute jumpers with a twist, etc. Men's wear and accessories too.

Miu Miu (16) The younger, fresher more directional diffusion line of trend-leader Miucca Prada. Miu Miu for girls with an interest in brilliant, eye-catching, seasonal pieces. Quirky light and pure fashion.

Charles Jourdan (17) Patrick Cox continues the tradition of foxy, elegant shoes for this long-established fashion house. Head for the classic French pieces here – great for quality, and good for channeling a Catherine-Deneuve-in-the-1980s look.

Carine Gilson (18) Very sophisticated silky lingerie

Patrick Cox (21) Shoes, of course. Fun, colourful, English irreverence – a holiday from French shopping

Sergio Rossi (22) Sexy Italian killer shoes for the unapologetic woman. Less fashion, more power.

Bruno Frisoni (24) Ex-Christian Lacroix designer's shoes with an edgy aesthetic

Editions de Parfums Frederic Malle (37) Exclusive perfumes made by the elite noses of the industry. The intimate, masculine-looking shop is as tasteful as you'd expect, designed by Andrée Putnam's protégée.

Christian Louboutin (38) This shoe shop is red, red, red, like the famous soles. Another footwear hero who is as sexy as Jimmy Choo but never cheap and trashy. His designs range from classics to experimental, artier pieces, and he still collaborates with young designers despite the fact that he's now part of the French fashion establishment.

THE HUB OF THE 6TH

The quintessential shopping streets for Parisian chic are to be found sandwiched between the long boulevard Saint-Germain and rue de Vaugirard. It's great to lose yourself on these small, narrow, winding roads, stopping off for a jumbo-sized macaroon at Ladurée (see Snack) or take a break from shopping to stroll through the wonderful Jardin du Luxembourg. The boutiques range from 'refined-chic' with the likes of Joseph and MaxMara to 'hip-chic', with the famous Lagerfeld Gallery, A.P.C. shops and retro-inspired Paul & Joe.

RUE BONAPARTE

Mona (17) Bohemian chic with pieces by the likes of Chloé, Alaï and Lavin
Ladurée Bonaparte (21) Macaroons that'll give you such a sugar rush you'll shop and never drop
Mandarina Duck (51) Contemporary wallets, bags and luggage from Italian designers
Swarovski (52) Lavish costume jewellery made from quality crystals
Princesse Tam Tam (53) Lingerie, swimwear and PJs for the young at heart
Comptoir des Cotonniers (59) France's answer to Zara. Wardrobe basics that are chic and affordable.
Cacharel (64) The luxury brand's biggest store, with ever funker designs (no more boring floral shirts) for women, men and children
Joseph (68-70) Chic and classic women's wear for both daytime and evening. A fantastic range of coats.
Pierre Hermé (72) Technicolour cakes – the signature *millefeuille* with pistachio cream is a must.

RUE DES SAINTS-PÈRES

Debauve & Gallais (30) Chocolate shop set in an old 18th-century apothecary

Paul & Joe (62) Hip designer Sophie Albou's clothes with a retro feel

Barbara Bui (67) Not avant-garde, but slick, classy and understated... this line is also popular in New York as a wardrobe for a working woman

Sabbia Rosa (73) Colourful satin, silk and chiffon negligees and lingerie

OTHERS

APC, *3 and 4 rue de Fleurus* Timeless wardrobe staples in a cooler, pricier French version of Gap. Great jeans for men and fun accessories that are slightly trendier than the clothes.

Camper, *1 rue du Cherche-Midi* Spanish shoes that are comfortable and eccentric

Lagerfeld Gallery, *40 rue de Seine* Karl's own brand. Good for jerseys, great tops and stretch pieces, all for people who can afford to splash out on rather anonymous items. Save your money for his much more interesting 7L bookshop a stone's throw away.

Lundi Bleu, *23 rue du Cheche-Midi* Famous for their zip-up boots with pointy toes. The winter collection is what to go for.

SURPLUS APC, *45 rue Madame* APC lines from last season at 'discount' prices

THE MARAIS

Full of original and quirky one-off boutiques as well as designer staples and an endless array of cafés, bars and eateries, the Marais is one of the most interesting areas to shop in. It's also the only *quartier* in Paris where shops open on a Sunday, most preferring to take their day of rest on Monday instead. This means the area will be buzzing with life while the rest of the city seems a little dead. There is something of interest on almost every street so it's best to walk through the 4th arrondissement in a snake-like fashion, starting at rue du Temple by the Hôtel de Ville and ending at the beautiful place des Vosges by the Bastille. Shops start to thin out a little within the 3rd arrondissement, where large stretches are dominated by not-so-desirable wholesale handbag outlets. However, it's probably true that the crossing thoroughfares of rue Vieille-du-Temple and rue des Francs Bourgeois make up the most densely shop-populated strip.

RUE DES FRANCS BOURGEOIS

Abou Ad'Abi Bazar (10) Elegant, funky and affordable women's fashion
Kiehl's (15) High-quality beauty products from the New York brand
Comptoir des Cotonniers (33) Casual basics from a mother–daughter duo
Zadig & Voltaire (42) Elegant basics and funky club-wear
Barbara Bui (43) Not avant-garde, but slick, classy and understated... this line is also popular in New York as a wardrobe for a working woman.
A-POC (47) A-POC (A Piece of Cloth) is Issey Miyake's second line, focusing on quirky designs that are still comfortable and functional
Nickel (48) Philippe Dumont's beauty salon for men, with its own brand of beauty products

RUE VIEILLE-DU-TEMPLE

Nodus (22) Men's shirt specialist, from the classic plain white to graphic patterns and stripes
La Belle Hortense (31) Browse the bookshelves with wine glass in hand at this wine shop (and bar)-cum-bookshop
Martin Grant (44) The Australian designer's unfussy chic grey and black clothes are timeless.
Bookbinders Design (53) Luxurious to funky stationery including blank books, photo-albums and designer briefcases
Jamin Puech (68) Off-the-wall, original handbags with character
Manoush (75) Colourful girly clothes and accessories, including signature Dorothy-style sparkly shoes
Jean Marie Poinot (85) Very funky acrylic jewellery
Yukiko (97) Vintage fashion mixed in with pieces by off-beat contemporary designers
APC (112) France's chic answer to 'Gap', but more expensive and much funkier. Collections for both sexes.

OTHERS

AB33, *33 rue Charlot* Very girly, casual-smart wear from the likes of Vanessa Bruno. Accessories, jewellery and lingerie stocked too.

Food, *58 rue Charlot* Mouth-watering selection of cookery books from around the world

Miller et Bertaux, *17 rue Ferdinand Duval* Imaginative designers Patrick Bertaux and Francis Miller sell everything from clothes to jewellery and CDs. Some of their designs have made it to Colette.

Xuan-Thu Nguyen, *1 rue Ferdinand Duval* Off-beat designer makes beautiful, original clothes characterized by hand-made embroidery and geometric shapes.

Annick Goutal, *3 bis rue des Rosiers* Feminine and seductive, just how you'd imagine a perfume shop to be.

L'Eclaireur, *3 rue des Rosiers* Super-luxe, high fashion that's dark and romantic, so Dries Van Noten, Carol Christian Poell and Undercover… but there are still some cleaner designers, such as Sinha-Stanic. The other essential Paris shop stop, along with Maria Luisa and Colette.

Anne et Valentin, *4 rue Sainte-Croix-de-la-Bretonnerie* Stylish unisex eyewear from cool titanium to bulky frames

Free 'P' Star, *8 rue Sainte-Croix-de-la-Bretonnerie* Popular and affordable vintage clothing

Antik Batik, *18 rue Turenne* Young, colourful and quirky trends, great for day wear

Azzedine Alaïa, *4 rue de Moussy* Boutique and shoe store by the Tunisian designer loved by glamorous women of all ages

L'Eclaireur Homme, *12 rue Malher* The other essential Paris shop stop along with Maria Luisa and Colette. Designer clothes by the likes of Dior Homme and Dries Van Noten for men.

Issey Miyake, *3 place des Vosges* Innovative explorations of fabric by the inventive Asian designer

K. Jacques, *16 rue Pavée* St Tropez-made leather sandals – must-haves for the summer

Karine Dupont, *22 rue Poitou* Cool, casual day bags in many, many colours

Mamz'elle Swing, *35 bis rue du roi de Sicile* Vintage clothes, shoes and accessories

Mariage Frères, *30 and 35 rue du Bourg Tibourg* Tea shop and tea room by France's first importer of tea

Oxyde: womens, *7 rue Saint-Merri* Trendy young women's wear with a great selection of off-beat trainers and shoes

Shine, *15 rue Poitou* Multi-brand boutique that stocks different labels, from Cacharel to Cheap Monday

Shoe Bizz, *48 rue Beaubourg* Affordable reproductions of the latest trends

CANAL SAINT-MARTIN

The area around the Saint-Martin canal isn't really a shopping drag as such, but exploring the romantic leafy quai and the atmospheric surrounding streets of, what was once, an industrial working-class area is an unbeatable experience. Rue de la Grange aux Belles and Beaurepaire are good streets for shopping, along with the canalside itself. Small independent boutiques are waiting to be discovered, while a growing number of established brands are moving in as the area becomes more and more gentrified (Agnès b. and American Apparel are fine examples). It's an excellent place to find boho-chic fashion items and it has one of the hippest (and most famous) art and design bookshops (Artazart) in Paris. Have lunch at Le Sporting (see Eat), or a pizza snack at funky Pink Famingo (see Snack) or simply finish the day with an aperitif on the wonderful terrace of chilled Chez Prune (see Drink).

QUAI DE VALMY

Artazart (83) Trendy design, art, multimedia bookshop

Stella Cadente (93) Dress up as an electric fairy with this eccentric fluorescent girly wear

Antoine et Lili (95) Two boutiques dedicated to colourful clothes, accessories and home-ware with ethnic leanings

RUE BEAUREPAIRE

American Apparel (10) Sport and street wear from anti-sweat shop LA brand

Boutique Renhsen (22) Glamorous printed T-shirts and skinny jeans for boys and girls

Frivoli (29) New and vintage clothes

Ofr (30) Avant-garde design and graphic magazines and books

Potemkine (30) Fantastic collection of art house films on DVD and books on cinema

OTHERS

Agnès b., *1 rue Dieu* Modern classics for men and women

Viveka Bergstorm, *23 rue de la Grange aux Belles* Avant-garde jewellery that uses an array of materials along with the usual silver and gold

DEPARTMENT STORES

Le Bon Marché Rive Gauche, 24 rue de Sèvres
Tel: 01 44 39 80 00 www.lebonmarche.fr
Open: 9.30am–7pm Mon–Thurs; 10am–9pm Fri; 9,30am–8pm Sat

Le Bon Marché is more of a giant boutique than a department store. It's beautifully decorated (with the help of Andrée Putman) and very chic; the staff are plentiful and it never seems as crowded or as hectic as Printemps or Lafayette (bear in mind that this is relative and the sales are a nightmare everywhere, especially at Christmas). Dating back to 1848, it's the oldest department store in Paris, where designers from Chanel to Helmut Lang can be tried and (cough) bought. Any foodie should visit the enormous food hall, La Grande Épicérie (24 rue de Sèvres, open: 8.30am–9pm Mon–Sat), next door, although you may have to battle with the old ladies of the 6th, who will shamelessly queue-barge. Just within the sliding entrance doors to La Grande Épicérie is an escalator – use this as the easiest way to access the younger (less expensive) lines such as APC, Paul & Joe and Comptoir des Cotonniers on the first floor. You'll also find the Delicabar, where you can snack on anything from cake and coffee to hot savouries and salads on the fabulous terrace.

Drugstore Publicis, 133 avenue des Champs-Élysées, Champs-Élysées

Tel: 01 44 43 79 00 www.publicisdrugstore.com
Open: 8am–2am daily

Before its renovation and transformation was completed in 2004, the 1970s décor of this Paris institution seemed disorderly, dated and drab. Now, with its new steel and glass façade, its sparse interior and stylish contents, Publicis has managed to imitate concept stores such as Colette, only attracting a slightly larger clientele of tourists and business folk. On the ground floor there is a pharmacy, beauty counter (complete with Kiehl's products), glossy newsagent, tabac, bookshop (with English titles) and a very good deli (with extremely good pastries). Downstairs are wines, cigars, chic souvenirs and snazzy stationery. The bright brasserie is now a top stop for shoppers, and has a hip new look, with colourful airtex cushions and fluorescent jellyfish lights. The annexed restaurant, Le Marcel, is more for those interested in 'fooding' than shopping. But the best thing about Drugstore Publicis is its long opening hours.

Galeries Lafayette, 40 boulevard Haussmann, Grands Boulevards

Tel: 01 42 82 34 56 www.galerieslafayette.com
Open: 9.30am–7.30pm (9pm Thurs). Closed Sundays.

Galeries Lafayette looks a touch tacky from the outside, a fact not helped by the row of independent stalls selling cheap souvenirs and accessories (although they come in handy for an inexpensive beret and gloves set in winter). Inside, under the magnificent Belle Époque glass dome ceiling, is a different matter, however. It comprises four buildings: Lafayette Homme (menswear), Lafayette Gourmet (food), Lafayette Maison (home-ware) and Lafayette Mode (fashion). The first floor of Mode has a fantastic selection of designer jeans and hip designers such as Agnès b. and Et Vous. Otherwise, there is pretty much everything, from the *prêt-à-porter* lines of YSL, Gaultier and Givenchy to lesser-known, up-and-coming designers. Overlooking Paris, on the 6th floor of the main store, is a wonderful self-service restaurant where you can eat throughout the day, as well as a sushi bar, café and a champagne bar. In close competition with Printemps, right next door, Lafayette offers small extras, such as personal shoppers and free fashion shows on Wednesday afternoons. Unless you want to suffer a nervous breakdown, it's best to avoid this shopping Mecca in the run-up to Christmas.

MARKETS

Paris is home to an abundance of markets ranging from specialized antiques to bric-à-brac, gourmet foods to staple fruit and veg, and high-end vintage clothing to jumbled junk. Don't get put off by the rows of cheap tat that usually proliferate around markets – persevere for the quality stalls that are a touch further in towards the centre of the mêlée. For a comprehensive list, go to: www.paris.fr. Otherwise, here are some of the most famous.

Marché aux Puces Clignancourt, avenue de la Porte de Clignancourt, Paris North
Open: 7am–7.30pm Sat–Mon

Don't come here expecting to find a long-lost Picasso for €10. Everything's very expensive and the antique dealers know their stuff. But it's worth coming just to explore the glorious labyrinthine maze that it is (it's actually about ten markets in one) and toy with the idea of buying something large and impractical for the journey home. You will find genuine articles here (many antique shops sell beautifully restored pieces), along with the usual bric-à-brac. Some of the stalls sell a good range of vintage clothing too.

Marché aux Puces de Montreuil, avenue de la Porte de Montreuil, Paris East
Open: 7am–7.30pm Sat–Mon

This is where people in the fashion industry come for inspiration. You have to rummage through mountains of second-hand rubbish to find anything good, but you could find a real gem for €1! Some retro stalls have done the searching for you, but this comes at a price (€50+). Look out for the stall with funky-coloured cowboy boots. Otherwise, there are stalls and white vans selling bric-à-brac, an unusual amount selling uniforms and overalls (along with the usual army gear), and others selling fake Adidas T-shirts and tacky mobile phone accessories, etc. Make sure you buy some tat from one of the eccentric old ladies, who creatively display their wares on dirty blankets by the roundabout!

Marché aux Puces de Vanves, avenue de la Porte de Vanves and rue Marc Sangnier, Paris South
Open: 7am–7.30pm Sat–Sun

Unlike Clignancourt, you are likely to pick up a bargain here. It's also smaller, less confusing and more laid back. On sunny days strolling down the tree-lined street, stopping off to listen to some vintage vinyl or to try on an array of 1920s hats, is a real joy.

Marché Raspail , Boulevard Raspail – between rue du Cherche-Midi and rue de Rennes, St Germain
Open: 8.30am–2pm Sun

The organic food market that attracts posh Parisians (including many celebrities) and tourists alike. Most goods should survive the trip home with you, fantastic natural soaps (your suitcase will never have smelt so good) and bottled scented water, home-made jams and pots of honey. Otherwise, it's simply great to stroll up and down the market, sampling the bits and pieces many of the stalls have laid out for you to try. You can also have breakfast or lunch on the go, as many stalls serve up ready meals ranging from crêpes and hot chocolate to vegan galettes, roasted chicken and Mediterranean salads. It gets incredibly busy, so be prepared to queue!

Shopping List

play...

The organisers of French sport have not been having the best of times of late. First of all Paris unexpectedly lost out to London in the race to hold the 2012 Olympic Games, and more recently the jewel in the French sporting crown, the Tour de France, already tarnished by repeated drug scandals, was shamed by the disqualification of the 2006 winner Floyd Landis for drug use.

Having said that, France remains a force to be reckoned with on the world sporting stage. They reached the final of the 2006 football World Cup and are one of the favourites to win rugby union's equivalent competition on home soil in 2007. And as befits a sporting powerhouse such as this, the capital city has a myriad sporting facilities at the disposal of the visitor. Or if you would rather let other people do the hard work while you watch, there are no fewer than 33 sports stadia around the city.

Paris, of course, plays host to several major sporting events each year. Early on, the national rugby union team play their home games in the Six Nations Championship at the Stade de France. A little later, in May, Roland Garros holds one of tennis' four major tournaments (the only one to be played on clay). And every summer in July the Champs-Élysées sees the finish of the most famous

race in cycling, the Tour de France. Details of major sporting events appear in France's best-selling national sports paper, *L'Equipe*. Additional sources of information are the numerous posters that are put up around the city, and the relevant section of the weekly *Pariscope* magazine. Tourist offices are also a useful first port of call, and can provide maps and pricing information.

If you would like to get active yourself, Paris is also very well equipped. There are many gyms around the city that can be used on a pay-per-visit basis. These range from the basic to the luxurious, with the facilities of the grand hotels sitting at the top of the pile. Equally, there are numerous tennis courts and swimming pools that are open to anyone and well maintained. If you want to combine tourism and exercise, bicycle hire shops allow you to discover the city in this way. And although Paris is not a city blessed with large green spaces at its centre, a short métro ride will take you to the open expanses of the city's two main parks, the Bois de Boulogne and the Bois de Vincennes, where there is enough space for almost any sporting activity imaginable.

Local information on sports facilities is posted on the town hall's dedicated website www.sport.paris.fr (there is an English-language version online), and much of the same information appears in *Le Guide du Sport à Paris*, which is a free booklet available from tourist offices. The website not only has listing and pricing information but also a useful interactive map to allow you to find sporting facilities in your area.

BOULES

This is a variation on the British game of bowls, usually played on a small area of gravel. The players throw the heavy metal ball at the jack (the *cochonnet*, literally 'piglet') from a crouching position and points are scored on the basis of whose ball lands closest to it. If you would like to watch, or even participate in, this most French of games the best places are the Place des Arènes de Lutèce (5th arrondissement) or the Boulodrome in the Jardin du Luxembourg (6th). Further information is available from www.petanque.fr ('petanque' is another word for boules).

CASINOS

There are no special restrictions on casino-type gambling in France, and there's a number of good establishments in and around Paris. You should be aware that while it is possible just to turn up at a casino and play, you need to take your passport with you in order to do so. It is also best to dress smartly, as some casinos do not allow jeans or trainers. There will also sometimes be an entry charge to the games room. Tables tend to close at 4am. These are a couple of the best places to go and try your luck.

Aviation Club de France, 104 avenue des Champs-Élysées, Champs-Élysées
Tel: 01 45 63 32 91   www.aviationclubdefrance.com

Open 24 hours a day, seven days a week, this wood-panelled club could not be more central. It offers blackjack as well as poker and backgammon for a table charge. There is no roulette, however. Non-alcoholic drinks are free, and there is a restaurant and lounge bar where you can spend your winnings.

Casino Barrière d'Enghien-les-Bains, 3 avenue de Ceinture, Enghien-les-Bains
Tel: 01 39 34 12 91   www.lucienbarriere.com
Open: 10am–4am (tables open 4pm–4am) daily

Situated in the outskirts to the north-west of the city, this is the region's largest casino. It is in a pretty location next to a lake, and the main rooms are ornate and date from 1901. There are 24 roulette tables as well as poker, blackjack and punto-banco. A modern extension houses 350 slot machines. Restaurants, bars and a theatre complete the complex.

CLIMBING

Paris boasts excellent facilities for this minority sport, although you should be aware that you need to obtain an ID card to use any municipal climbing wall. You should take your passport and insurance documentation with you the first time you want to climb. Paris' largest climbing wall, with 1,350 square meters to scale, is at Mur Mur Pantin (55 rue Cartier Bresson, Pantin; tel: 01 48 46 11 00, www.murmur.fr; métro: Aubervilliers). This complex is open seven days a week and use of the wall costs between €7 and €13. The staff here will be able to point you towards alternative facilities.

If you are after a real rock face, then Fontainebleau, only a short distance south of the capital, has ascents to suit all abilities. Full details and visitors' information are available from the Club Alpin Français de Fontainebleau (tel: 01 64 22 67 18, http://caf77.free.fr).

CYCLING

As mentioned in the Introduction, the most gruelling race in the sport of cycling, the Tour de France, has had its reputation sullied in recent years by continuous doping scandals. This, combined with the fact that the French have not had a home winner to cheer since 1985, might tempt you to think that the Tour was losing its appeal. This is not the case, however, and each year in July the French public line the 3,500km covered by the world's best cyclists in pursuit of the famous yellow jersey. You can find out about the history of the Tour, along with information about next year's course and competitors, on the race website, www.letour.fr. In terms of witnessing the event for yourself, while the race's outcome is invariably decided in the gruelling mountain stages, you can go and see the high pomp of the finale at the end of July on the Champs-Élysées, where the successful riders are greeted by the French president and the winner is crowned before a crowd of hundreds of thousands. The sides of the great avenue are lined with seating for the great and the good, so don't expect to get too close to the action (although the atmosphere alone is worth the trip).

If you want to get into the saddle yourself, you'll find Paris has an extensive network of cycle paths, which make this a practical and enjoyable way to see the city. This is a good solution to the problems of the often over-crowded métro and the shortage of taxis. Most cycle lanes are marked in white on the dark asphalt. Care is required, as many of these lanes run adjacent to the traffic. More user-friendly are the cycle lanes marked in blue, as these are separated from the flow of vehicles. A map of the city's cycle paths can be found in the free Paris à Vélo brochure, which is available from the town hall and tourist offices as well as some hotels and bike hire shops.

There is, however, no getting away from the fact that Paris is a congested city. If you want to get away from the traffic altogether your best bet is to head for one of Paris' two main parks, the Bois de Boulogne in the west (métro: Porte Maillot, Porte Dauphine) and the Bois de Vincennes in the east (métro: Chateau de Vincennes, Porte Dorée). Both of these parks contain many miles of cycle lanes, at weekends and public holidays they are closed to the traffic. Bear in mind that it might be difficult to squeeze your cycle onto the métro, and that you might be better off just cycling there.

Cycling in the centre of town also becomes easier on Sundays and public holidays, when the town hall's 'Paris Breathes' initiative dictates that many roads are closed to motorized traffic. Again, details are available at the tourist office.

There are several places around town where you can rent a bike. Prices generally include the loan of a helmet and lock and seem to be between €15 to €25 for a day, or around €60 for a week. You will need to leave a deposit either in the form of your passport or your credit card details. These are a few good hire shops:, which are listed below.

Fat Tire Bike Tours, 24 rue Edgar Fauré, Invalides
Tel: 01 56 58 10 54 www.fattirebiketoursparis.com
Open: 11am–5pm daily

This company not only hires out bikes and but also organizes various English-language bike tours, leaving from the base of the Eiffel Tower. For the less energetic, they also offer innovative Segway tours.

Gepetto Et Vélos, 59 rue du Cardinal Lemoine, Latin Quarter
Tel: 01 43 54 19 95 www.gepetto-et-velos.com
Open: 9am–1pm, 2–7.30pm. Closed Mondays.

This shop rents out bicycles as well as selling BMX and Chopper-type cycles.

Paris à Vélo C'est Sympa, 22 Rue Alphonse Baudin, Oberkampf
Tel: 01 48 87 60 01 www.parisvelosympa.com
Open: 9.30am (9am Sat/Sun)–1pm, 2–6pm (7pm Sat/Sun). Closed Tuesdays.

This company hires out bikes and organizes themed tours of the city, both by day and by night. They can also provide tandems.

FOOTBALL

Football in Paris, as in most European capitals, is the most popular sport. And in recent years the French national team have rewarded their fanatical supporters with much success. Having won the World Cup on home soil in 1998, they went on to win the European Championship in 2000. Most recently they reached the World Cup Final in 2006 where a moment of madness by their captain and talisman, Zinedine Zidane, cost them their chance of victory. Home games are played at the huge 80,000 seat Stade de France (Saint-Denis, 16th; tel: 01 55 93 00 00, www.stadefrance.fr; métro: RER La Plaine-Stade de France). The stadium was built to host the 1998 World Cup Final. If you fancy going along, check the website for a fixture list and ticket information.

By way of league football Parisians are largely limited to Paris-Saint-Germain, a club set up only 35 years ago to sate the capital's need for a top-flight football club. They play their home games at the monolithic concrete structure of the Parc des Princes (24 rue du Commandant Guilbaud, 16th; tel: 01 49 87 29 29, www.psg.fr; métro: Porte de Saint-Cloud). It is possible to get tickets to see the team play for as little as €15. If you want to go along, you should call the above number or navigate to the ticket section of the website. As PSG is Paris' only top-level football club, it's necessary to book early as the games are understandably popular.

If you want to kick a ball about yourself, you should head out to either the Bois de Boulogne or the Bois de Vincennes, where there are always plenty of kickabouts going on. In addition, the town hall sometimes erects temporary five-a-side pitches on the Champ-de-Mars in the shadow of the Eiffel Tower. These can be booked, and sometimes casual competitions are staged. More information about these facilities is available on www.sport.paris.fr.

GYMS

Paris is a city where looking good is at an absolute premium, and therefore gyms are common. There are many establishments offering a wide range of facilities and classes. Some places try to get you to commit to a long contract, but others are happy to let you pay on a per-visit basis. If you want to stay fit but resent paying for it then check out the Town Hall's 'Sport Nature' initiative, which organizes free outdoor gym classes in 12 locations around Paris. They run on Sundays from 9am to midday throughout the year (except July and August). Further details are available on www.sport.paris.fr. In terms of paying gyms, the following offer good facilities.

Club Quartier Latin, 19 rue de Pontoise, Latin Quarter
Tel: 01 55 42 77 88 www.clubquartierlatin.com
Open: 7am–midnight daily

This club, housed within a 1930s building, offers a swimming pool, four squash courts and gym facilities and classes. Entry to the gym costs €19 per day, or €151 for 10 visits. It's close to the university and therefore popular with students.

Espace Vit'Halles, 48 rue Rambuteau, Beaubourg
Tel: 01 42 77 21 71
Open: 7.30am–10.30pm Mon–Fri; 9am–7pm Sat; 10am–7pm Sun

This centrally located gym next to the Pompidou Centre has been voted one of the best gyms in Europe, and has great facilities and a wide range of classes. It is open until 10.30pm during the week and during the day on Sundays, which is unusual. Fees are €25 per day.

Ritz Health Club, 1 place Vendôme, Louvre
Tel: 01 43 16 30 60 www.ritzparis.com
Open: 6.30am–10pm daily

This club is modelled on a Roman bath and features the most up-to-date gym equipment and the deepest swimming pool in Paris (4m) as well as a sauna, hammam, jacuzzi and massage cabins (Swedish massage, shiatsu, Vichy shower massage). At €150 per day it is clearly expensive, but it is the most luxurious place in town.

HORSE-RACING

You can find details of the race meets, which take place at the seven race courses around Paris, in the dedicated racing paper Paris Turf. The Bois de Boulogne is home to the city's two main racetracks. The most glamorous is the Hippodrome de Longchamp (Route des Tribunes, Bois de Boulogne, 16th; tel: 01 44 30 75 00; métro: Porte d'Auteuil and then free shuttle bus). This course hosts the greatest day of thoroughbred horse-racing in Europe on the first weekend in October. This is the most important day in the French racing calendar, with the highlight being the famous Prix de l'Arc de Triomphe. A little further south lies the Hippodrome d'Auteuil (address: Route des Lacs, Bois de Boulogne, 16th; tel: 01 40 71 47 47; métro: Porte d'Auteuil). This is Paris' top steeple-chasing venue and is host to the Grand Paris steeplechase every May. If you would like to watch a trotting race, often a pleasant thing to do in the evening (when they are run), then head east to the Hippodrome de Paris-Vincennes (2 Route de la Ferme, 12th; tel: 01 49 77 17 17; métro: RER Joinville-le-Pont).

Tickets for the races tend to cost between €2 and €8. Further information on these and other race–courses as well as a full racing calendar is available on www.france-galop.fr.

Betting on the horses is a little more complicated in France, and you may be surprised by the complete absence of bookmaker's shops in the city. This is because, while there is not an outright ban on this type of gambling, a law dating from 1891 required the industry to be run under a state-associated monopoly to avoid mafia corruption. This means that all books in France are run by Pari-Mutuel Urbain (PMU), a company set up in 1930 by the President to fulfil just this role.

Therefore if you fancy a flutter you will have to head for one of the many bars or cafés that display the green 'PMU' sign outside. You should be aware that while a wide range of bets is open to you, when it comes to horse or trotting races (the most popular being a three-horse wager called the 'tiercé'), it is not possible to bet on the outcome of other sporting or general events.

ICE-SKATING

You can ice-skate almost all year round (Sept–June) at the Patinoire Sonja Henie in the Palais Omni-Sports de Paris-Bercy. It is open every day – check the website for details. The rink measures 500 sq. m, and entry ranges from €4 to €6 depending on when you go. This does not include skate hire, which costs €3. You can also hire helmets and knee and elbow guards for €1 per item.

In the wintertime (Dec–March) the town hall pays for several spectacular ice rinks to be set up around the city. They also lay on free music. These rinks are free to the public but skate hire will set you back about €5. And even if you do not intend to skate, the rinks are certainly impressive enough for you just to go along to enjoy the scene. The largest of these public rinks, measuring a huge 1,200 sq. m, is on the Place de l'Hôtel de Ville (métro: Hôtel de Ville). The site is particularly atmospheric in the evening when the buildings all around the square are illuminated. Next in size is the 800sq.m rink by Paris' tallest building, the Tour Montparnasse (place Raoul Dantry, 15th; métro: Montparnasse-Bienvenue). Most spectacular of all, however, is the 200 sq. m rink suspended between two legs of the Eiffel Tower and offering breathtaking views across the city. There might be a queue, since only 80 people are admitted at any one time; but on the plus side entry and skate hire are included in the admission price to the Tower.

JOGGING

The Paris Marathon takes place every April and follows a circuitous route starting from the Champs-Élysées. Many people line the route and there are live music performances at various spots along the way. If you want more information, or want to participate, go to the website (www.paris-marathon.com). Athletics meetings take place in the Stade de France (see

Football, page 233, for details) and at the Palais Omni-Sports de Paris-Bercy (8 boulevard Bercy, 12th; tel: 01 46 91 57 57, www.popb.fr; métro: Bercy).

If you fancy something a little less committed, www.sport.paris.fr has details of the city's various running tracks, which can be used for a small fee. Equally, despite the congestion, there are various routes that are favoured by joggers. In the centre of town the embankments of the Seine and the perimeters of the Champ-de-Mars and the Jardin du Luxembourg are popular, as is the Jardin des Plantes. Or again, a little further afield the city's two main parks, the Bois de Boulogne and the Bois de Vincennes, are excellent for a scenic run.

If you want to run in a group the Hash House Harriers, a group who describe themselves as a drinking club with a running problem, offer weekly outings in various locations around the city – catch up with them on www.parishhh.free.fr.

ROLLER-BLADING

If you would like to enjoy a leisurely skate at your own pace then head for the Left Bank of the Seine on Sundays from 9am to 4pm. The stretch from the Musée d'Orsay to the Eiffel Tower is full of 'bladers enjoying themselves. If tricks and ramps are more your thing, Les Halles, the place du Trocadero and place de la Bastille all contain adventurous youngsters finding unintended and novel uses for the municipal furniture.

Every Friday sees Friday Night Fever, a three-hour group skate running from 10pm to 1am, which attracts literally thousands of young, trendy rollers. It is organized by Pari-Roller (16 boulevard Saint-Germain, 5th; www.pari-roller.com; métro: Saint-Germain-Des-Prés). The skate usually leaves from the place Raoul Dautry near the Tour Montparnasse (métro: Montparnasse-Bienvenue), although you should check the website as it is subject to cancellation or alteration due to weather conditions. The standard, and speed, of those taking part are very high so you should probably steer clear if you are a novice. There have also been complaints that the marshals may not speak English and can be a little rude if they feel you are not up to the requisite standard. On the plus side there are no traffic worries as the police close the route of the skate to cars. It is free to take part but you can choose to pay a subscription that includes insurance.

A more relaxed daytime group skate is organized on Sunday afternoons by Rollers et Coquillages (23 Rue Jean Jacque Rousseau, 1st; tel: 01 44 54 94 42, www.rollers-coquillages.org; métro: Les Halles). Again, this is free of charge, and the pace is less frenetic, but the route can be hilly so they emphasize that you should be good at breaking. There are marshals to help you along.

There are several places around town where you can hire skates and safety equipment. These are a couple of good ones.

Roller Location Nomade, 37 boulevard Bourdon, Bastille
Tel: 01 44 54 07 44 www.nomadeshop.com

They provide a wide range of rollerblades to suit all abilities. Prices start from €8 per day and €30 per week. They can also give lessons.

Vertical Line, 4 rue de la Bastille, Bastille
Tel: 01 42 74 70 00 www.vertical-line.com

A wide range of skates going up to very large sizes. A day's rental costs €10, and this includes safety equipment. It is open every day but closed on Monday morning.

RUGBY

Like the national football team, the French rugby side play their home games at the Stade de France (Saint-Denis, 16th; tel: 01 55 93 00 00, www.stade-france.fr; métro: RER La Plaine-Stade de France). Although locals complain that the huge, 80,000 capacity stadium does not quite have the boiler-room atmosphere of the team's previous home, the Parc de Princes, going to see France play rugby in front of their own supporters is still a great experience. Normally the highlight of the year will be the home internationals in the Six Nations Championship, running from January to March. In 2007 this will be upstaged, however, as France plays host to the rugby World Cup. Tickets for such games sell out very quickly, and subsequently change hands for many times their face value. More information about games and tickets is available on the French Rugby Federation's website (www.ffr.fr).

In terms of domestic rugby the capital's top team is Stade Français, which plays its home games at the small (12,000-seat) Stade Jean Bouin (26 avenue du General Sarrail, 16th; tel: 01 40 71 71 00, www.stade.fr; métro: Porte de Saint-Cloud). They do, however, use the Stade de France for some of their bigger games. They have been national champions several times in recent years but European glory seems to always just elude them (they've been runners-up twice in the Heineken Cup).

If you want to get involved with a team yourself you should contact the British Rugby Club of Paris (58 avenue de la Grande Armée, 17th; tel: 01 40 55 15 15, www.brfcparis.com; métro: Argentine). This club, founded in 1923, is open to all nationalities and prides itself on its friendly, inclusive environment. They put out two sides every Saturday during the season and there is also a more casual 'folklorique' side, who play more occasional fixtures.

SPAS AND HAMMAMS

In Paris, vanity is no vice, and you will notice an *institut de beauté* on almost every corner, offering an array of treatments from your standard plucking to more outlandish oxygen pumping. There is also a surprising number of hammams (steam baths) in the city, offering beauty treatments and massage. These do not operate, as in the UK and US, as a veil behind which the practitioners of the oldest profession carry on their business. Rather, they mimic traditional Arabic hammams and are calm places to unwind with a cup of mint tea, sauna and a traditional massage. The sexes are generally segregated but most places do offer mixed sessions, so just ask. There are occasional nudist afternoons but in general the modesty of the clients is protected by a small loincloth, which is provided (swimwear must be worn at mixed sessions).

L'Appartement 217, 217 rue Saint-Honoré, Louvre/Palais Royal
Tel: 01 42 96 00 96 www.lappartement217.com
Open: 10am–7pm daily

The name alone will give you the impression that you've been given secret address to eternal youth, and you won't be far off-track – having been in charge of the 'beauty corner' at lifestyle store Colette, Stéphane Jaulin, knows his stuff. He's chosen to concentrate on treatments using primarily organic products, such as the Dr Hauschka range (try the absolutely incredible 'Hauschka' full body massage, 1h30, €95) as well as sci-fi treatments from Japan (the anti-ageing infra-red sauna, €740). You are given a towel (warm) and some tea (Ayurvedic) before being exposed to the sweet scent of natural essential oils and a rather funky soundtrack (thank goodness, no more new-age pan-pipes). Dark floorboards and colourful painted walls offset by white orchids complete the modern look. The place has been so feng shui-ed you can't help but feel at blissful ease.

Les Bains du Marais, 31 rue des Blancs Manteaux, Marais
Tel: 01 44 61 02 02 www.lesbainsdumarias.com

This chic establishment has a Middle Eastern themed interior and is a very pleasant place to enjoy a sauna and massage in elegant tiled surroundings. It costs €35 to enter the steam rooms and another €35 for a massage and *gommage* (a rub-down with a special rubber glove). Various beauty treatments and products are also available, and there is a decent restaurant. You should phone or check the website for opening hours and session times.

Hammam des Grands Boulevards, 28 boulevard de Bonne-Nouvelle, Grands Boulevards
Tel: 01 48 01 03 05
Open: 12.30–10pm (8pm Fri). Mon–Fri; 12:30–9pm Sat–Sun. Closed mid to end of August.

This hammam is located in the basement of a large building and is decorated in dark wood with a 1950s fountain as its centrepiece. There are two steam rooms, a plunge pool, a rest area and a café as well as massage facilities. The atmosphere is friendly but you should phone ahead, as some sessions are nudist.

Nickel: Male salon, 48 rue des Francs Bourgeois, Left Bank
Tel: 01 42 77 41 10 www.nickel.fr
Open: 11am–7.30pm (9pm Wed–Thurs). Closed Sundays.

Philippe Dumont was so tired of having to put up with girly gossip magazines, pink robes and long, hard stares, he opened his own beauty salon exclusively for men. Here you can indulge yourself (or be indulged) with anything from a relaxing massage (1hr, €50) to love handle liquidation treatment (€50) or a full body wax (ouch!). The staff are friendly and good-looking (obviously) and there is a huge range of beauty products you can buy to continue the miracle work at home (including a Nickel own brand). This being Paris, men walk in and out without a hint of embarrassment (but rather with pride) – so follow suit!

Nuxe Spa, 32 Montorgueil 75001, Louvre
Tel: 01 55 80 71 40

A candlelit 'Californian' massage by a dark and handsome stranger to the soundtrack of Massive Attack – what more could one ask for? It's so relax-ing it's hard not to dribble all over the couch. The Nuxe Spa is recessed behind a courtyard off the rue Montorgueil, held back from the street like a closely guarded secret. Its beige and brown interior is minimal but warm, with canvas-tented therapy rooms, exposed dark wooden beams and lime-washed brickwork. The whole place smells comfortingly like honey, an ingredient Nuxe features in its products. The stylish staff are very friendly and put you at ease, and there are therapists for face, body and soul – one of whom works at the Aqua Spa in the Sanderson Hotel, London, during the week. Without even opting for one of the 'slimming' treatments, one can't but leave feeling several years younger and lighter, turning heads with one's glow.

UMA: Massage and Yoga, 14 rue Choron, Montmartre
Tel: 01 44 53 61 13   www.uma-paris.com
Open: 10am–7pm (6pm Sat). Closed Sundays.

On the chic side of New Age (if there is such a thing), you'll find no tie-dye fabrics or dangling dream-catchers here. Rather, bare pink walls, light pine floorboards, a library stocked with the usual array of lifestyle guru books and a small tearoom where you can sip an Ayurvedic tea or get a herbal remedy fix. The slogan at UMA is L'art du mouvement et du bien-être ('the art of movement and well-being'), probably because you can practise yoga not for just one hour but for four hours at a time (that's a lot of movement,

€35), as well as experience the innovative 'Gyrotonic' yoga technique (which involves a machine much like you'd find in a medieval torture chamber – only it's supposed to be good for you). They also take massage extremely seriously here, using techniques from all over the world (India, China, Thailand, Japan). Try the Indian 'Pichauli' (€100) where two sets of hands rub you down with warm essential oils. Pure heaven.

SWIMMING

You are not allowed to jump into the Seine for a dip, but despite this the undoubted highlight of this section is the Paris Plage programme, which turns a stretch of the Seine embankment by the Pont Neuf and Notre Dame into a beach for the months of July and August. Thousands of tons of sand, together with a few palm trees, are used to create the effect. The aim of the initiative is to bring summer to the few Parisians who cannot leave the city at this time of year. Anyone can go along to grab a sun lounger, and more recently a 28-metre pool has been added in response to complaints that there was nowhere for the assembled sun-worshippers to cool down.

Further up river you will find another novel swimming spot. The Piscine Seine-Est (Port de la Gare, Quai Françoi-Mauriac, 13th; tel: 01 44 68 12 12, www.paris.fr; métro: Bibliothèque François Mitterrand), in the shadow of the National Library, is actually suspended in the water of the Seine. The pool is open from 10am to 10pm and costs €5 for a 2-hour visit. The main pool measures 25 x 10m and there is also a 50 sq. m paddling pool. There are two large sundecks, one of them on the roof of the pool itself, as well as a sauna, café and gym.

If you crave a more conventional swimming experience, Paris is very well equipped, boasting no fewer than 35 municipal pools. There's also a number of more expensive private establishments. All pools require you to wear a swimming cap, and men must wear Speedo-type swimming trunks as opposed to the Bermuda shorts type which are much more popular in the UK and US. Entrance to public pools is set at €2.60 and you can get a 10-visit multi-pass for €21.50. More information is available on the town hall's website, www.paris.fr, which also gives opening times. You should be aware that public pools are often closed on Mondays for school visits.

Piscine Butte aux Cailles, 5 Place Paul Verlaine, Buttes-Chaumont
Tel: 01 45 89 60 05
Open: 7am–7pm Tues–Sat; 8am–6pm Sun

Housed in a wonderful red brick Art Deco building dating from 1924, this small complex contains a 33-metre indoor pool. Diving and water aerobic facilities are available but the highlight is the 25-metre outdoor pool filled with naturally warm water from the 600 metre artesian well at the site. The pool is not ideal for lap swimming, however, as it can get quite crowded.

Piscine Georges Vallery, 148 avenue Gambetta, Belleville
Tel: 01 40 31 15 20
Open: 11.30am–1.30pm Mon; 11.30am–1.30pm, 4.45–10pm Tues/Thurs; 10am–5pm Weds; 11.30am–5pm Fri; 9am–5pm Sat–Sun.

This pool is a little away from the centre but is certainly worth the trip. It boasts a large 50 x 21m pool and a retractable Plexiglas roof so that it can be in use all year round. There are sun beds, a bar area and a children's pool. Johnny Weissmuller, the original Tarzan, used to come and train here.

Piscine Pontoise/Club Quartier Latin, 19 rue de Pontoise, Latin Quarter
Tel: 01 55 42 77 88 www.clubquartierlatin.com
Open: 7am–midnight daily

This pool is in the very heart of the Latin Quarter and is popular with students from the nearby Sorbonne University. This can make the atmosphere either rowdy or flirty depending on the day. The interior is a gem of Art Deco design, with mosaics, columns and original brass fittings. A glass roof lets in natural light. On week-nights the pool is open till 11.45pm for evening sessions.

Piscine Roger Le Gall, 34 boulevard Carnot, Reuilly
Tel: 01 44 73 81 12
Open: noon–2pm, 5–8pm Mon/Tues/Thurs/Fri; 8am–-9pm Weds/Sun; noon–7pm Sat

This 50-metre indoor pool is a little far from the closest métro station. It is home to the Club des Nageurs de Paris and therefore the approach to swimming is generally a little more serious. Again, there is a retractable roof, and you can sunbathe on the lawn in the summertime.

Piscine Suzanne Berlioux, 10 place de la Rotonde, Forum des Halles (level 3), Marais
Tel: 01 42 36 98 44
Open: 11am (10am Weds)–10pm Mon–Fri; 9am–7pm Sat-Sun

This underground swimming complex beside the landmark Pompidou Centre is one of Paris' most central, and yet it still contains a 50-metre pool. To make the aquatic experience more pleasant the windows on one side of the hall give onto a lush tropical greenhouse. The pool has reopened after a refurbishment programme in 2006.

Also available is the privately owned Aquaboulevard swimming complex (4 rue Louis Armand, 15th; tel: 01 40 60 10 00; métro: Balard). This enormous pool is perfect for children – it has wave machines, waterslides, mock beaches and tropical islands. And there are saunas and cafés where parents can seek refuge.

TENNIS

The second grand slam tennis tournament of the calendar year, and the only one to be played on clay, takes place every year in May at Roland Garros in south-west Paris (Stade Roland Garros, Porte de Mousquetaires, 2 avenue Gordon-Bennett 16th; tel: 01 47 43 48 00, www.rolandgarros.com; métro: Porte d'Auteuil). Thanks to the surface the matches tend to be long and gruelling, while the crowd can quickly turn against non-European players, giving the tournament an added edge. It is hard to get tickets for the show courts and to do so (legitimately) you must enter the postal ballot, details of which are available on the tournament's website. General tickets, which allow you to wander around the non-show courts early in the tournament, are easier to obtain and can generally be bought on site on the day if you get there early enough. These tickets are also sometimes available via the website.

If you want to play yourself, use one of 41 municipal tennis centres in Paris, although most of them are on the small side. Slots can be booked online at www.tennis.paris.fr once you have registered and received a username and password. Open courts can be used for €6.50 per hour while covered courts, where available, cost €12.50 per hour. It is also possible to buy a reduced 10-visit multi-pass. The most central, but probably the most crowded, courts are the six in the Jardin du Luxembourg (tel: 01 43 25 79 18; métro: Luxembourg). The largest tennis centre is the Suzanne Lenglen Complex (2 rue Louis-Armand, 15th; tel: 01 44 26 26 50; métro: Balard), which has 14 courts, two of which are covered.

info...

HOLIDAYS

Rod Stewart said something once about the French never working. He was right. Everyone takes a two-week holiday in August, but the majority of restaurants, bars, clubs and shops will shut for the whole of August. One could say that things start to quieten down after the exhausting celebrations of Bastille Day (14 July). AVOID Paris in August – it is a ghost town (unless, of course, you like that sort of thing). There are bank holidays practically every week in May (when the shops will be closed). Sunday is a day of rest, so shops and many cafés and restaurants will be closed then too.

MÉTRO

Trains run from 5.30am to 1am. Look out for the amazing Art Nouveau signs, or the modern equivalent, which is a large yellow 'M'. The métro is by far the cheapest, and easiest, way to travel around the city. A métro map is vital, so make sure you pick one up from any station ticket office (it's free). Remember to keep your used métro ticket with you at all times: just because you don't need it to get out of the station doesn't mean there isn't a grumpy inspector waiting to catch you out (playing the dumb tourist doesn't always work). Best to throw it away only once you've physically left the métro. You can buy a carnet of 10 tickets (so 10 single journeys) for €10.70, which you can use on both the métro and the buses.

MONEY

The currency is the euro (€). A credit card is called a 'carte bleu', 'CB' for short, so watch out for signs saying 'Pas de CB' ('No credit cards'). Try to avoid the bureaux de changes, as you will always get a better exchange rate from a bank or by withdrawing at ATM machines.

SMOKING

Smoking is synonymous with Parisian life, although now bars and restaurants must have designated non-smoking areas by law, and all public spaces (shops, banks, railway stations, etc.) are non-smoking. Cigarettes can be bought in tabacs (you'll be able the see the iconic sign outside). Most of these are closed on Sundays, although many bars and brasseries sell cigarettes too.

i

info...

TAXIS

It isn't easy to hail a cab on the streets of Paris, so you have to make your way to designated taxi ranks (dotted around the city and marked with a blue sign). It's a good idea to keep a detailed map with you, as the cabbies here don't have the Knowledge (in fact they often don't have a clue where they're going). There is a minimum charge of €5.50, but usually a trip in central Paris costs around €7–15 (be warned: if they insist on putting your tiny weekend bag in the boot, it's because there's a surcharge for 'luggage' at €0.90 per piece). You can always dial a cab, but be aware that you also pay for the time it takes them to get to you.

Taxis Bleus, tel: 01 49 36 10 10, www.taxis-bleus.com

Taxis G7, English: 01 41 27 66 99, French: 01 47 39 47 39

TELEPHONE

The international dialling code for France is +33. The local code for Paris is 01. Make sure you drop the '0' when dialling France from abroad, i.e: +33 1

TICKETS AND TIMETABLES

Entertainment listings can be found in the Wednesday supplements of major newspapers and the weekly magazines *Pariscope* and *L'Officiel des Spectacles*. All these are in French. For an English-language listing of all cultural goings-on, visit www.parisinfo.com: it gives all the box-office telephone numbers and online booking links. To avoid the larger museums' hellish queues, get a Paris Museum Pass available from participating museums or tourist offices (2 days: €30, 4 days: €45, 6 days: €60); it gives you unlimited access to the permanent collections. For club listings see the music magazine *Trax*.

TIPPING

You are not expected to tip in Paris (there's already a compulsory service charge added to your bill). This is great when it comes to moody or down right abusive waiters or taxi drivers. But it's a hard life and if you can afford it and the service is good, why not be generous? (Note that Parisians will always round up their bill.)

Notes & Updates

Notes & Updates

Notes & Updates

Notes & Updates

index

index

253

index